IN DEFENSE OF THE AMERICAN TEEN

"An insider's commentary on the state of our secondary schools"

RYAN TEVES

authorHOUSE®

AuthorHouse™
1663 Liberty Drive
Bloomington, IN 47403
www.authorhouse.com
Phone: 1-800-839-8640

First published by AuthorHouse 7/22/2010

ISBN: 978-1-4520-1919-2 (e)
ISBN: 978-1-4520-1917-8 (sc)
ISBN: 978-1-4520-1918-5 (hc)

Library of Congress Control Number: 2010907605

Printed in the United States of America
Bloomington, Indiana

This book is printed on acid-free paper.

A special thanks to all of the families I have served, having taught me more than I could ever teach them.

Most of all, a thanks to my own beautiful family. "My family is not rich by any means, but I feel as though I've won the lottery." - The Format

Contents

INTRODUCTION

FOR A PERSON TO BEGIN a task like writing a book, there certainly has to be a source of inspiration. The inspiration has to be grand enough to keep the alleged author going, even during the inevitable dry times that will threaten the completion of that book. For this project, I certainly wasn't lacking in inspiration, as I live the topic at hand and was given fresh material daily. My career as a teacher and a tutor was the soil in which this work was grown.

It seems that the vast world of education, specifically, but not limited to, secondary education (high school and middle school) has long sought an insider to speak to the rest of the world about its inner workings. Hold your applause, but I have accepted the position.

With just the title of "teacher," I feel as though one would be qualified to discuss the strengths and weaknesses of education in America today, but my specific situation might make me hyper-qualified. While I am a certified science and math teacher for middle and high school, it is the fact that I have been involved in the other more alternative corners of education that gives me a more of a broad perspective on what is going on.

For the sake of merit, this is where I list my experience in education. I have taught at a catholic all girls private school, I have taught at four different public schools in two different states, both in summer school and the regular year, I have taught at a home-school collective, a continuation school, and probably most importantly, have run my own tutoring business for five years in both Hawaii and California. Each experience, I've noticed, has shed just a little more light on what education is, and thus I feel as though I have really developed a comprehensive understanding of the complex animal.

The aim of this book, originally, came from my desire to defend the teenagers from my tutoring program, that were unfairly labeled as "bad kids" by teachers and school administrators, but a sort of evolution has taken place during the work. A task as simple as making a case for why these kids are being wrongly labeled took turns into the deepest dusty corners of education in America, and just as a mechanic operates, the correction of one problem inevitably led to the discovery of another. Along these lines, this book came together.

Regardless, it is with my funny and outstanding tutoring kids in mind that I present this book to the world. Never mind what the petty notes of a frustrated school official may have eluded to from time to time, these kids range from outstanding athletes and artists, to brilliant academic scholars and future leaders. It is my sincere hope that the daily frustrations of teaching in the public school system do not impede the ability or interest of our teachers, including myself, to inspire and encourage these students. All kids are different, and this simple and elegant truth should be celebrated rather than frowned upon. If there is not sufficient flexibility in our school systems for unique individuals to flourish, it simply needs an overhaul, and an overhaul is precisely what is recommended and offered in this work.

So read on and if the stories and anecdotes don't pertain to your own child directly, they just may pertain to your experiences as a student yourself when you were in high school. Hollywood and kids themselves portray high school as being anything but inspirational and usually depict teachers as either horribly mean or completely complacent. While the characters in these movies are dramatized for humor or to make a point, it is a fact that many reflect on their time in school in this way. The reality is that school does have some major flaws; your child might not just be venting.

The focus, again, though is on secondary school as this is the area of my expertise, but also because it is here that the problem is most dire. In doing research on our competitiveness on the world stage, as well as in holding simple discussions with the kids themselves, it is apparent that our elementary schools are largely successful, while our secondary schools are lacking. This is not only the case with statistics and our success in reference to other nations, but in how our kids view their educational experience. Elementary school kids are largely content with and excited about what they are learning, while our middle and high school students express an entirely different sentiment.

What was of invaluable worth to me was the fact that, while I am a secondary school teacher, a good friend of mine has been teaching elementary school for several years. Through our many and varying discussions ranging from curriculum to the willingness of our kids to learn, real and tangible differences were made clear between the elementary school experience and the elementary mind and that of their older counterparts. The two worlds are very different, as my friend and I discovered, and unfortunately, one seems to be largely working while the other is not. This is a theme in this book that will be visited and revisited and explains much of the teen angst that we see in our kids.

But rather than have a negative tone, I consider my understanding of school to be good news for parents and for our kids. The take home message, in most cases, is that our kids are not failing, as their report cards might suggest from time to time, but that school has become somewhat abstract and many times irrelevant. Your kids are likely witty, funny, creative, and tenacious and deserve to wear positive titles, rather than negative ones. This is the focus of this work.

CHAPTER I: SECONDARY SCHOOLS ARE BROKEN

IT IS NOT UNCOMMON FOR parents to spend a bulk of their time with their teenagers discussing and, frankly, fighting about school. From grades to the completion of homework, school, during middle and high school, has taken on an almost entirely negative tone. And while there are obviously exceptions to this rule, the majority of parents are forced to either fight with their kids to keep them active in school, or simply give up the cause. And because most parents value education and see it as a stepping stone to future success, the fight continues.

In contrast, though, for things that the kids are interested in, away from school, this same struggle doesn't exist. Many kids participate in constructive activities, such as sports, music, or work, and so it is not the case that all kids are simply apathetic. As is the case with adults as well as kids, we actively engage in things that we find interesting or inspiring, but resist those that seem irrelevant or pointless to us. Unfortunately, school hasn't sold itself to many of our kids.

Although increasingly so, the same isn't entirely true during the elementary years. During K-5, the tone is largely positive around school, and both student and parent enjoy the successes around realistic and enticing challenges. It seems as though both the curriculum and rigor are close to what is being sought by elementary kids, and thus, there is not tremendous struggle in our elementary schools. Kids seem to genuinely want to learn to read, write, and learn simple arithmetic, as they see their adult counterparts using these skills on a daily basis. In short, it is not hard to find an elementary kid that will gladly state "I love school." Finding a high school student that will make a statement like this is less likely.

But if our younger kids are so engaged in learning and have such an inner desire to succeed, both to impress their parents and for personal growth, what happens to our kids overnight, as they enter secondary schools? And while there is a certain amount of physiology behind why teenagers are defiant in nature, our secondary schools seem to bring out the worst in our kids.

The reason that there is so much frustration amongst parents and students in our secondary schools, and frustration between students and teachers, is that our secondary schools simply don't offer what our kids need and are seeking. When a parent is faced with just their individual child and his or her struggles, they assume that a problem has arisen with them. What I propose is that the problem is not with the kids themselves, but that the problem lies in our secondary schools. From what I've seen through tutoring and teaching is that our kids are still the bright and optimistic individuals that they were through elementary school, but just that they've been put in an almost ridiculous situation. Our secondary schools really can be ridiculous.

CHAPTER 2: EVIDENCE THAT SECONDARY SCHOOLS ARE BROKEN

THE TWO LARGEST CATEGORIES OF evidence that show how our secondary schools are struggling are found in the sentiment of the students in middle and high schools and in the actual statistical analysis of our American secondary schools performance worldwide. Depending on one's perspective, either of these categories may hold more weight or importance, but they are both significant and paint a picture of a system that isn't working.

With regards to the sentiment of our students in the middle and high schools, as described above, one only need ask a student of these places how he or she feels about school. While there will be exceptions, the majority of kids will state that they simply don't like school or that they like their friends, but don't like the academic side of school. At best, kids seem to consider school to be a necessary evil that has been prescribed by their parents or school administrators. The students who are successful treat school as a chore and get it done, while kids who need more inspiration simply begin to fail.

The reason secondary schools stand out is in the evidence that the struggle is isolated to just these years, from grades seven through twelve. Not only do elementary schools not show the same problem, but college is equally loved by its students, and reports from kids in college are largely positive. Most will describe their college experience as a time of intense learning and incredible personal growth. With the freedom of choice and the determination of one's own direction, children enter adulthood and largely find only positivity in college.

So if one were to interview our students, their description of their entire time in school, from elementary school to college, it would go along the lines of; great – terrible – great. We need to address this period of a lack of personal satisfaction in our students during middle and high school.

The statistical performance of kids in elementary school, secondary school, and college versus the rest of the world supports the above. Just as contentment with school falls off during secondary schools, so do test scores and relative performance. Our elementary schools and universities are celebrated for their success worldwide, while our secondary schools lag behind the rest of the world.

Maria Glod, a staff writer with the Washington Post, in the article "U.S. Teens Trail Peers Around the World on Math-Science Test," 12/5/07 explains how American kids score relatively low on academic exams. The article states "On the science portion, U.S. students, most of them 10th-graders, received an average score of 489 on a 1,000-point scale, 11 points below the average of the 30 countries. Canada, Japan and Korea were among the countries in which students outperformed U.S. counterparts. U.S. students were on par with peers in eight countries and outperformed those from five others.

In math, only four countries had average scores lower than the United States. Students in 23 countries had a higher average score, and those in two countries did about the same as the Americans."

While this report is not news to anyone, as we have heard headlines along these lines for years, what is interesting is the pursuit of an explanation for these results. If our kids are successful in elementary school and in college, why are they doing so poorly in secondary schools? More importantly, are these poor results due to some flaw in our kids or are they due to the schools themselves?

Unquestionably, it is the latter, but the reason has nothing to do with the bandwagon that everyone seems to enjoy jumping on.

CHAPTER 3: REASONS THEY ARE BROKEN

THE REASONS THAT SECONDARY SCHOOLS are not working, either in terms of educating our kids or inspiring them, seem to lie in four basic but broad categories. And obviously, with all of the discrepancies between schools and districts from state to state, the issues are complex and varying, but large fundamental problems seem to be consistent to all schools. Secondary schools may be losing the attention and passion of our kids at such an alarming rate because of these four basic flaws:

1. The curriculum of secondary schools lacks relevance.
2. Secondary schools do not allow for individualization.
3. Our middle and high schools have developed a ridiculous workload and process for evaluation.
4. The schools themselves are intensely inefficient.

The funny thing is that the first three of these issues come from the direct reports of the teens themselves, as kids of all shapes and sizes have expressed the same concerns. While not all kids are equally articulate, they have had the same complaints. From A students to D average kids, they all explain that "this stuff will never help me in my life," and that "this homework is way too much." I have heard these same complaints from kids for years, the complaints make sense, yet no one appears to be listening to them. I listened and I agree.

CHAPTER 4: CURRICULUM ISN'T RELEVANT

I'M SURE READER, THAT YOU excel at something. It may even be reading, which, if you possess that skill, you know to continue through rough spots of a book with the confidence that the writer will find their way again and excite you once more. But I digress, what are you good at? Whatever it is, I have a feeling that you had some participation in the choosing of that activity. That is, you probably applied for your job or filed your business name with the county. It is unlikely that you were handed a hobby or job and the person said… "Enjoy this and do well at it." Sure there are things in our lives that we do because we are responsible adults, like wiping the seat after we pee (men, you heard me,) and paying bills on time. But for the things that take passion to be successful, we pretty much pick our path. Well, the reason that teen-agers have always written songs about misery and being misunderstood is because for them, the concept of choosing their own path is certainly not a reality.

Kids are given seven subjects, none of which are their choice, and are told to be enthusiastic. And if you think that drama or woodshop is a choice for a teenager that likes punk rock, I'll let you choose between reading manuals to microwaves and filing folders in a doctor's office. It is nearly impossible for a bureaucrat in Washington DC to approximate the interest of kids across America and then to assign courses along these lines. So, by definition, it is no easy task to create and maintain relevant classes, but as a rule, if an elective has been around since my grandfather's sophomore year, we might want to revisit its' practicality. The current index of classes or electives in no way parallel the experiences in life that we value the most.

Because many kids are not drawn by the standards, curriculum, and list of courses in secondary school, this is where the misdiagnosis of our kids begins. If a student does not embrace what is offered in school, they are accused of being apathetic or of not being interested in learning.

One of my favorite kids was rewarded for his apathy in school with a call to his mom. In the discussion the teacher said that her son doesn't have the desire to learn. The funny thing is, that kid practically blows my hair back with questions about things from politics to wealth and everything in between. The kid does nothing but seek knowledge and learning, just not in the arena of adding fractions and analyzing Shakespeare. He seeks learning that is relevant to his life and will undoubtedly be extremely successful as an adult. Suggesting that this kid did not have an interest in learning is precisely the inaccurate labeling of our kids that I intend to correct.

The beauty in reading and learning as adults lies in our ability to pursue the knowledge that we are thirsty for at that very moment. If I have in interest in incorporating my business, the next book that I read will be on that subject, however, in other points of my life I might have been seen reading books on woodworking or real estate. Kids do not enjoy the same luxury.

I once heard a business man say that the most expensive commodity in the world is not gold, or oil, but information. This is absolutely true, and I even believe that kids subscribe to this same fact. There is a discrepancy, though, between what kids want and need to know, and the information that makes up the bulk of our standards and curriculum in secondary schools.

Right now the typical high school curriculum goes essentially like this. Every kid has to take two years of math to graduate, but must take at least through Algebra 2 to apply to a competitive college. Every kid must take two sciences, typically biology and physics or chemistry. Then of course you have English, History, Physical Education, a foreign language, and the required amount of arts to graduate. The arts offered at the school in which I work are ceramics and painting. Now, I get the fact that all kids need to learn arithmetic and how to read and write, but the above list isn't exactly dazzling in its ingenuity.

Just as an example, English classes should not be boring or seem irrelevant to kids. Book sales around the world are in the millions and millions of dollars, so apparently reading is something that humans enjoy doing. Teenage girls line up around the block to buy and read the "Twilight" series, so why is there such apathy in English in school. Irrelevant curriculum is that answer.

Rather than debate which book is better for kids to read, allow them to choose their own book. This is how we do it as adults, and everyone wins. My wife and I don't read the same books and I can only be thankful that no one has mandated that we do.

Math and science, two of my favorite subjects, might be even more guilty of employing irrelevant curriculum. It would be a startling number if I were to have tallied how many times kids asked "how is this going to help me in my life," while doing their science and math homework. The reality, unfortunately, is that much of the math and science curriculum will not be useful to them in their real lives.

To best illustrate this, I have put together a short compilation of problems from the homework assignments of these very kids. The list of problems was randomly taken from required courses in high school, including math, physics, and chemistry and were absolutely not chosen because they are hard and would prove the point more readily. These are legitimately normal problems from mandatory high school classes. Look at them and tell me if you even have the slightest idea how to solve them.

Then, more importantly, ask yourself if the understanding of these problems could help you to reach your goals in any way, financial or otherwise. Now, there are people in the world who can answer these, but most are teachers. And even amongst teachers, most can only answer the questions in their subject matter. The chemistry teacher will likely get the chemistry one right and the math teacher will get the math right. Beyond that, only the kid is expected to know all subjects.

It is not only unlikely, but almost an impossibility that even the principal of the school would be able to pass the finals of all of the required classes for graduation, from English and Spanish to Chemistry and math. In fact, the president of the United States of America would likely also not be able to accomplish this task. With this being such an obvious truth, why are standards from the state and federal governments accepted with little or no fight? Before secondary schools are to become truly successful, this issue of curriculum being absurdly irrelevant needs to be completely corrected.

EXAMPLES OF HIGH SCHOOL CURRICULUM
PHYSICS, CHEMISTRY, AND MATH QUESTIONS

---

1. How many moles of Fe2O3 are present in 1000 kg of the oxide? Atomic weights: Fe, 55.8, O, 16.0

2. A dry-cleaning solvent has a molecular weight of 146.99 g/mole that contains C, H, and Cl. It is suspected to be a cancer-causing agent. When a 0.250g sample was studied by combustion analysis, 0.451 g of CO2 and 0.0617 g of H2O was formed. Find the molecular formula of the solvent.

3. A 0.513 g sample of a compound containing only carbon, hydrogen, and nitrogen burns in excess O2 to produce 1.04 g of CO2 and 0.704 g of H2O. Calculate the mass percent of N in the compound.

4. Find the coordinates of the vertex of $f(x) = 4(x-1)^2 - 3$ Without graphing, determine if the vertex is the maximum or minimum point of the quadratic function.

5. Factor: $3x^2 + 7x + 2$

6. Solve for X and Y: $x - 2y = 14$ and $x + 3y = 9$

7. Determine the value of the variables:

$$x + y + z = 22$$
$$2x + y - z = 40$$
$$-x + 10y - 2z = -12$$

8. A 15,000 kg rocket launcher holds a 5000 kg rocket. The rocket exits the launcher at +450 m/s. What is the recoil velocity of the launcher?

9. A 1325 kg car traveling north at 27 m/s collides with a 2165 kg car moving east at 17 m/s. As a result of the collision, they stick together. What is their velocity after the collision?

The End

How did you do? Not to be mean, but I don't even really have to ask. Again, the aim here is not to make you feel the anxiety that probably accompanied your childhood come test time, but to make a point. Knowledge and education are the most powerful and wonderful things in the world, but out of context, they are worthless.

And for the parents that only feel compounding frustration by my little quiz and statements thereafter, and who can't change how schools are run, I only offer this advice. Just try to understand why your kid is not thrilled about acing these classes. Empathy is what is called for. If your angle has been that there is something wrong with your son or daughter, that angle is not only unfair but totally wrong. If you disagree, I am going to need you to send me the results of the quiz you just took. Ha ha, just kidding.

We learn best when we have the question before we seek the answer. To rephrase, if you attend a class on working on transmissions, you might not get a lot out of it. But, if the transmission goes out in your car and you intend to fix it yourself, and then you see the class advertised in the paper and you attend, you will take up that info like a sponge. Along these lines, curriculum needs to be individualized so that the kids have some say in what information is laid out in front of them. If they desire the information offered in a certain course, they are much more likely to burn through that material.

If you are trying to find holes in my discussion, I have one for you. If none of these kids have to take these difficult math and science classes, who is going to build our shuttles and find out if there is life on a distant planet? Great question, but it'll take more than that to slow my stagger.

How about the flip scenario? The US is pretty much the leader in rock & roll and rap. If we don't push all kids to do it in school, will we lose our lead? The answer is that not all expertise needs to be hand-fed to all kids. We will always have individuals with vastly different interests that become experts in the field to which they are drawn. We apparently decided that a certain amount of math is needed to build shuttles, and then made the absurd jump in logic that every single kid in America should have to learn that math, regardless of the kid's affinity or ability in the subject. Our kids need to be allowed to specialize, ensuring that curriculum will always seem relevant to them.

In a discussion with one of my students one time, we got on the topic of the relevance of curriculum and decided that every chapter in a math book should have to list what job would use that chapter's material. Unfortunately, we came to the conclusion that "math teacher" might be the only example for most chapters.

Go ask a banker which chapter pertains to his profession. Go ask a general contractor the same question. These professions certainly use math to be successful, however, they use a tiny portion of all math in existence and specialize on those few types of problems. Everyone, at some point, needs to specialize to become successful. I think that specialization happens too late in life in America.

And to defend math, there are certainly, without question, issues in math that all students should understand, and many of them are difficult. Fractions, percentages, a certain amount of trig and geometry are applicable. It is absurd to suggest, as some kids sarcastically do, that math can or should be eliminated. This being said, though, the content required now is too much and too abstract. Much of the math we teach to kids today is useful only in a purely academic sense.

I asked a math major at the local college what she was going to do as a career, she pondered for a moment, much like she does when finding the double derivative of a function, and answered, "I guess I'll teach math." You are darn right. What else is she going to do where her random collection of math knowledge will serve a specific purpose?

And for the students who genuinely do enjoy learning the more abstract concepts in math, they shouldn't be discouraged from doing so. Rather, I would want to nurture that love for math and offer it in a pure format to those kids. I would love for those kids to have pride in their excitement for math and would love to have them surrounded by similar peers, in a small class size, learning at as quick of a rate as they desire. It is a disservice to those kids who love math to fill the desks around them with kids who, fairly, don't want to be there.

I have sort of unfairly cornered English and math as the only guilty subjects with regards to curricular irrelevance, but the trend is real for all subjects. Growing up, I loved animals and plants and eventually went on to major in molecular, cellular, and developmental biology in college for that reason. Useful or not, I really believe that spending time analyzing the natural world is never a waste of time. But like most of the kids in America today who are accused of not wanting to learn, I only excelled in the topic that got me thrilled. I wonder, though, if I were attending today's secondary schools if I would have been drawn to science with the same passion. Science, unfortunately, has also moved toward the drowning of concepts in details.

We should all know the kingdoms. We should all know that matter is made up of tiny particles too small to see. But do we all have to know how many valence electrons are in the atom with the atomic number of 35? We should all know that plants provide animals with the essential ingredients for life, and vice versa, but should all kids know the infinitesimally small details of every step of photosynthesis?

There is more discussion of the phases of mitosis than there is the beauty of the concept of mitosis. Mitosis is how an animal can start as a single tiny cell and end up eating fruit from branches twenty feet high, but our kids are only taught and tested on the obscure differences between each little tiny step in mitosis, like Anaphase and Metaphase. The danger inherent in cramming more and more standards into one course or subject like biology is that the kids are drowned in details and fail to see the beauty of life and how it propagates.

High school is the place to plant seeds and to generate genuine curiosity and a love for learning, and is a place for our kids to begin to lean in one direction or another. It is a time of personal growth for many kids, and most important, a time to find some sense of self. Kids are looking for passions and identities at this age, which explains the high volume of different hair styles over a short period, and high school should be used to introduce them to neat ideas and concepts. It is certainly not a time to turn them off from subjects due to an over-use of dry and useless detail. Biology is a wonderful subject, and any teacher that presents it as anything else should be ashamed of him or herself.

All subjects should be brought up in an attractive and engaging manner and then kids should follow their path based on which subject brings them the most success and fulfillment. Kids in high school are not too young to begin to specialize, but that direction should be self-imposed rather than dictated by a teacher or administrator. If they are drawn to a subject, they should begin to ask questions along those lines and to consider majoring in that topic in college.

And to defend the teachers, even where a teacher means well, they are slaves to standards. I suppose it would be unfair to blame biology teachers and teachers of other subjects today for this compiling of more and more detail into one subject, as they are indeed obligated to follow the standards requirements set forth by the state and federal governments. When I mentioned to an administrator the above concern, she stated "well you work for the state." Many have become complacent in the pursuit of steady and unquestioned pay.

So, in the discussion of schools today and why there seems to be a fundamental failure in secondary education, much of the problem begins here. Without relevant curriculum our kids will likely be disappointed, and we as a nation will likely feel the same sentiment. Standards are the bedrock upon which our schools are being built, so this is where we need reform.

Chapter 5: Curriculum isn't individualized

To look at the broader picture, the current format of our secondary school curriculum is not even consistent with our American ideals and entire way of life. We often celebrate the notion that we all have different passions and interests and we enjoy that we have the liberty to pursue those passions. It has never been argued that all people should strive to accomplish identical goals or that there is some uniform path to success that we all must follow. In other words, there is no standardized test that we all take as adults.

In contrast, though, secondary schools do just this, even while our kids are beginning to enter a phase of life in which they are developing the desire to identify self. The aim to put all of our secondary school age kids into the same box is not necessarily cruel in nature, but simply does not work with human nature or with the developmental stage that young teenagers are in. This concept is similar to an intriguing statement my professor in college once said, stating "communism is the best form of government, but it simply doesn't work with human nature." The same is true of seeking the same outcome from all of our young.

So, in seeking a reason for why secondary schools are likely so unsuccessful, this issue can't be cast aside. In fact, of the multiple problems with secondary schools, this might be the largest. Our teens are desperate to individualize, but are not allowed to in school. The comment "I hate math," is an inarticulate way of stating that they understand that they have no use for finding the asymptote of a graph, and would like to develop expertise in other areas. As long as we both deny and fight the concept that humans, beginning in the early teens, seek to develop specialty, we will always fight an uphill battle.

Nowhere is this point of the inability of a student to individualize more clear than in the discussion of whether a kid is failing due to a lack of ability or affinity. Upon meeting new students through my tutoring program, my first question is always the same. "So, do you like school or do you hate it?" Based on their response and what weird design they twist their face into, I can tell right away. Our kids are crying out for the ability to specialize and it is time we listened to the audience that we are so interested in helping.

Chapter 6: Affinity vs. Ability

IT HAS TRADITIONALLY BEEN so difficult to put a finger on why a student is struggling, because there is not always a clear line between ability and affinity. Academic ability is one's inherent or genetic ability to complete academic tasks and to solve academic problems or questions with ease. Ability is akin to a processor in a computer, in that without a focus on what software has been downloaded onto the computer, how strong or fast is the processor.

Affinity for a subject, on the other hand, is merely a measure of one's love for that subject. If a person is passionate about something, they have a high affinity for it. Maybe not surprisingly, the latter of the two is a much stronger determinant for success, but we can't ignore ability when designing policies that expect the same results from all kids.

Just as there is variation among individuals of all species, as Charles Darwin made clear in his explanation of the evolution of species, there is certainly variation amongst us as humans. As uncomfortable as it may seem, some kids simply have an easier time learning math and other academic concepts due to some innate ability, while their counterparts may not. The old expression "we are all the same on the inside," is absolutely incorrect. Our DNA, unique to every human being, directs all cell activity, and so our propensities for certain diseases, our physical structure, our circulatory system, the effectiveness of our immune system, the function of our brains, and every other biological function in our body will completely vary from person to person. This notion of variation is a certainty in the medical field and is not controversial.

The plan for education today seems to propose that we expect the same results from all kids, regardless of inherent ability or affinity in or for a given subject. This policy of expecting all students to perform the same on standardized tests and the enforcements of rigid state and federal academic standards for every kid are just not plausible and have been part of a failed policy from the day it was conceived. Then, in an attempt to find a mean or average for all kids on these tests, the bar has been set too low for high achieving students, and too high for kids that are struggling, thus the policy has the result of serving no one.

Rather than trying to suppress the reality that there is a discrepancy amongst inherent ability, what if we were to face it head on? It is ridiculous to give a kid who burns through math like a fire through pine needles the exact same expectations as a kid who legitimately struggles with simple math concepts. Not only is it absurd, but it is a gross waste of resources. If one were to calculate the extra resources it takes to attempt to bring a kid who isn't naturally able in math to the same level as a student who is gifted in math, the amount would be startling, while the goal isn't even a valuable one.

The reason this discussion of affinity versus ability is important to a parent, is that if one's kid is struggling, identifying which of the two is the culprit is the key first step in correcting that difficulty. The efforts of the parent have to be different depending on whether or not the student lacks the ability or lacks the interest in the subject.

For instance, as an example as to how I am able to deem that a student is naturally good at math, he or she might be able to do arithmetic quickly in their head, while others can not. For instance, a kid with D's in math but that is able to multiply 24 X 6 in their head is good at math. On the other hand, I have had many "A" students that simply can't do this level of math in their head, and because they are hard working and go about math in a methodical way, they get the answer just as correct after writing the problem out. I love when kids are able to complete the process correctly and am not critical of the fact that they don't do the work in their head, but their excellent grades don't indicate that they are naturally more gifted than the first kid in math. Again, the difference in grades is a result of effort or affinity rather than ability.

Unfortunately, more and more kids are joining the ranks of the disinterested, as the trend in academics is moving towards more and more detail, and less and less relevancy. Because of this, many kids are moving away from the more dry subjects. I have never met a kid, in today's academic climate, that states that they want to be a math major. In much the same way, fewer and fewer kids are professing their love for the sciences, as the focus has seemed to shift away from the macro subjects and towards microscopic details within disciplines.

Because of the fact that school has become much more than being about ability, or even effort, grades are reflecting the intelligence of the student less and less. There are so many extraneous factors determining one's grade in school today, that it really is hard to determine someone's academic worth.

The saddest outcome of an experience with learning is where a cluttered and unfair grading policy gives a student the wrong sense of self. Many kids genuinely think that they are average to poor math students, even though they probably found the math to be easy. But when a person sees the grade in black letters on a report card, it is hard, at such an early age, to simply dismiss it as an administrative anomaly.

So what to do if your kid is struggling? Again, the answer is different depending on whether the issue is a lack of ability or a lack of interest.

The good news is that the steps to take are more straight-forward in the event that a kid simply is less inherently talented in a subject. No subject is above any child, given time and patience, so a parent can easily employ a plan to bring the kid up to speed. For example, with math the parent can sit down with the kid, or have a tutor sit down with the kid if resources allow, and simply hover for every single problem. Then, where a specific math issue is unclear, the parent can add extra work in just that area, or take an aside to discuss that specific topic. In this painstaking manner, a parent can add the extra support that a kid might need.

For subjects other than math, again, a slow and thorough approach will certainly lead to better results. If a kid is struggling in History, for example, the parent can help the student to study by quizzing them on every pertinent fact until the information comes easy. Memorization is not hard for any student, regardless of ability, and is the key to success in many subjects like history, biology, and even Spanish. If a kid suggests that memorization is in fact hard, just cite the infinite number of songs that he or she can sing along to, without error. Memorization is merely a function of how many times we hear or say something. After a million times, any kid can tell you the dates of wars or the meaning of Spanish words.

For the kid that is less than talented in a particular subject, what is not an option is finding extra support with the student's teacher. There simply isn't the time in the day for the average busy teacher to be able to give the kid the extra support that they need. Many teachers may offer the token schedule of "office hours," but real change happens at home. Absolutely do not rely on just the school that your child attends to remedy the problems that arise with a lack of innate ability for a subject. Even in the case that a child is declared as being "special needs" and is allowed extra freedoms with regards to school work, this won't replace what can and should happen at home for extra reinforcement.

Unfortunately, the real life situation of many families doesn't cater to the plan mentioned above. That is, many parents simply can't find the time in the day to sit down with their kids for a couple of hours of homework per night. In addition to cooking, cleaning, and attending to whatever other siblings there may be, some parents don't consider the above to be possible. If that is the case, the only alternative is to have extreme patience with your child and, frankly, to not punish them for negative results from school. If a parent can admit that a plan for success exists, but that they simply can't afford to follow it, the blame, in my opinion, should shift away from the kid. It is hardly the fault of the child that the bar has been set too high for them, given their situation.

One of my students in the past was in the eighth grade and was reading at a second grade level. Although I was technically the math and science teacher for this student, I was particularly concerned with the reading. Even though I love the sciences and find value in math, neither can be considered as fundamentally important as the ability to read and write with proficiency, as these skills are a daily part of every adult's life. A conversation with this kid's parents shed light on the real issue with this type of kid.

When I mentioned the situation with the student's mom and stated that we had to take action, I was surprised by her response. I stated that the best way to learn to read is by picking up books from the nearest book shop, that are exciting to the kid, and to simply start reading them. The key is to let the kid pick the book out, regardless of content (within reason.) and if the book is exciting enough, the kid will continue to push through it. Then, the parent can hover and correct pronunciation and can even take turns reading with the student. This plan, I mentioned, was sure to eventually work, as it would be tough not to learn to read, if this happened every night of the week.

The mom responded by saying "Do you know how tired I am at the end of the day?" She went on "do you know how hard it is to have a kid like my son?" She basically laid out a case for me of why this plan was too demanding and of why she didn't think she should have to do it. When I persisted, stating that we as teachers don't have the one on one time to do something like this reading plan, she stayed firm.

So, in the above case, the mother made a decision that the effort needed for her son to progress was too great to put into action. This mother basically decided, in my opinion, to let her son face a lifetime of difficulty and struggle, because her role in his progress would be too demanding. A similar decision will have to be made by all parents of kids who actually struggle with a particular subject, from math to English or Spanish, and it will come down to how bad the parent wants success for their child. For my own children, the decision has already been made. If a subject is important, like reading, writing, or whatever we deem important as a family, it is our sole responsibility, and our responsibility alone, to make sure that our kids find success. Having worked in education for years, I absolutely understand that our teachers are limited in what they can do and no one, ultimately, is to blame for our kids' failures but us as parents.

We do have to pick our battles, though. As every family has a different set of goals or priorities, it may be that not every academic subject merits the same response. That is, if your child is struggling in art, you may feel as though a huge supplemental effort at home is not needed, whereas for a difficulty in reading and writing, it might be. Of course, another family might come to a completely different conclusion, but the fact still remains that real and effective change can only happen at home, in the cases where a child needs more than is being offered within the limited resources of school.

To cite an example that we are all familiar with, Barack Obama's mother reportedly offered a similar supplement to Barack's education early on, having faced the reality that he wasn't getting what he needed in school. When they, as a family, were living abroad, and Barack was attending an international school, his mother had him wake up at an absurd hour before school (as early as 4 a.m.,) to practice reading and writing in English. This was to ensure that, regardless of the level of education he was getting at school, he would be polished in his mastery of the English language. We can all speak to the results of her efforts, and attention has been paid to what it must have been like for Barack himself to go through such a rigorous program.

Where the attention should be directed, though, is towards his mother and what such a task required of her. It would have been extremely easy for her to label this type of supplementary education as too burdensome, and the temptation to sleep in and rely on the school to "do its job," must have been great. Never the less, Barack Obama's mother faced the simple reality that he wasn't getting what he needed at school and accepted the responsibility to ensure that her child be educated to a level that she deemed acceptable. All parents can learn from this lesson.

So, again, if your child is struggling due to ability, much can absolutely be done. I have never met a kid who couldn't learn, but some simply need more time and attention than others. But again, in some ways this can be considered to be good news, as difficulty of this nature can be overcome. What is more complicated, however, is when a kid struggles because of a disdain for the subject.

A whole different approach needs to be taken with the kid who has the ability but simply doesn't like school. First off, understanding and having the student understand that the bad grades and poor performance comes from a lack of interest rather than ability is particularly important. It is unhealthy and destructive to have a student say " I suck at math," or whatever the subject may be, and then, because this notion seems to be confirmed by bad grades, the parent doesn't disagree with them. Kids that I tutor are often surprised to hear that the kids who have A's in math are no better, inherently, at math than they are, but that the other kids simply have put forth more effort. This initial identification of the difference between ability and affinity is important for the self confidence of the student, but also is important in finding a solution for the problem at hand.

I can sincerely remember, in my own life, believing that the "smart kids" were simply better in math and better in school in general, than me. I believed this in the depths of my heart. Obviously with the difference in grades and the fact that they were being accepted to Stanford and Berkeley, they simply had some ability that I didn't. Only after I majored in molecular, cellular, and developmental biology in college, with success, did I come to the life altering conclusion that "hmm, I guess they weren't more inherently intelligent."

Just as I had to work tremendously hard in college to be successful, it became clear that these kids had likely tried very hard in high school to obtain those results. Obviously, I simply wasn't as interested in school at an early age, and I didn't put in the same effort that the excellent students did. It would have been nice, though, for me to have understood that truth then.

Once this notion that ability isn't the problem has been clearly laid out, a nonjudgmental discussion on the topic of school would be healthy for the kid and the parents themselves. Why not sit down with your kid and ask them what they do or don't like about school. The reality is that school does have some problems, and many of the complaints that the student might have will likely hold water. If your student complains that math seems to have no application to their real lives, arguing that they are wrong will lead nowhere, as much math in our state and federal standards in fact does have almost no application to our daily lives. Assuming that your child is lazy might not be the most productive way to move forward either. They may have a few good points.

Then, rather than focusing on what they don't have an affinity for and what they are struggling in, it makes a lot of sense to find what they do have an affinity for and push that. More specifically, if a child seems to not have an interest in history, but is passionate about biology, a parent would be wise to completely encourage their child to pursue biology, above and beyond school, while down playing their failures in history. Trips to aquariums and zoos, meetings with family friends in the field of biology, and or discussions with doctors about their career should happen outside of school, while the issue of how much the kid doesn't like history, should seldom come up.

Obviously the hurdle of history would have to be overcome, in the above example, and it may be math in other real life examples, but the point is that the focus of the family's energy should not be entirely on what the kid doesn't have an affinity for. There is always the option to help them extra in that subject, or to simply be less critical of a lower grade in that particular class. If a kid can't stand a subject and gets a C in that class, while achieving high grades in the classes that he or she enjoys, this can only be seen as a successful outcome, and is much the same outcome that you will see in your own life. If you love cooking and hate gardening, your meals will be wonderful and your garden will struggle along. We shouldn't fight the reality that humans succeed in the areas they have an affinity for, but rather we should celebrate that fact.

Then, in the not so uncommon situation in which a kid has no affinity for any academic subject or school itself, the same logic applies. For the kid who "hates" school, again, it is important to find what they do enjoy. There can always be something productive to be found in a person's life, even if it is outside of "the box." Fighting all day about school is counterproductive, if a young person has the interest in and the energy to pursue some goal away from school.

And to be clear, just because a kid doesn't like school doesn't mean he or she doesn't like to learn. Whatever the kid mentions as an area of interest can be pursued and pushed, ensuring that learning will happen. Likely, that learning will even involve a degree of reading and actual academic learning. For instance, if a kid is interested in computers, but hates school, a parent could begin collecting garage sale computers and let the kid tear them apart. The parent, again, could find people in the business to inspire the child, or could look for junior college classes along these lines. All of this would happen alongside normal school, but the discussions at home would turn away from arguments about the kid's failures and towards potential future successes.

The first response of a parent to this example might be that "my kid doesn't like computers... or anything," but this is absolutely wrong. Even if a child seems to only like "flighty" pursuits like becoming a famous rapper, encouragement in that direction is still productive. For the example of rapping, a parent could help the student get recording software that allows the recording of multiple tracks and could, again, find professionals in the music business to talk to the kid. Music software is very technical and requires cranial effort, and if the kid determines that the project is too hard, at least they have quenched that thirst and will likely move on. Encouragement in any direction, besides the obvious criminal or drug related pursuits, is always productive.

And the good news is that an affinity for certain subjects can come in different phases of our lives and does for most people. It may be that you, as an adult, have an interest in talk radio and listen to a particular station on your way to work. Maybe you feel as though it keeps you up on the news and is a productive way to pass the time in the car. Maybe you also feel as though listening to talk radio helps to develop your vocabulary and acts as a form of informal education. While these things are all true, it is unlikely that you were as excited about talk radio while in college. In college you may have scoffed at the idea of driving along in your car listening to talk radio. So, again, most affinities develop at different points in our lives. Just because your kid resents formal education now doesn't mean that this is a life long certainty.

So, again, the message for your own child is that it is impossible to force an affinity for a subject on someone, but through patience and a focus on success in general, your kid will thrive. Then, with the experience of finding success, no matter from where, they will likely tackle larger and larger challenges.

Moving the discussion away from the individual and to larger social trends, it is interesting to analyze which groups seem to "subscribe" to what school is, and are therefore likely to be more successful. From personal teaching experience, there seem to be very real trends of achievement and these trends seem to carry tremendous momentum. Unfortunately, working against these trends is very difficult. A focus on and an effort in school seems to be linked to socioeconomic cause above all else, with the students of the wealthy succeeding and the students from more poor families struggling.

This notion that kids who come from less wealthy homes appear to not do as well in school confirms further the concept that academic failure is more often a result of a lack of interest in school rather than actual difficulty. I can, with absolute certainty, make the claim that students from the continuation school in which I taught were not less intelligent than kids from my "excellent" class. Obviously on an individual basis, kids varied regardless of the class, but again, it was not true that the trend was that students that were freshman in geometry (largely successful,) were naturally brighter in math than my troubled seniors taking algebra.

So, why then do kids from certain backgrounds find success in schools while kids from other backgrounds do not. The answer lies in the simple truth that I discovered early in my teaching career and that has been brought up several times in this book. Parents, for better or worse, have a much larger impact on the academic future of their children than do teachers. It is extremely hard for a teacher to reverse fifteen years of a negative attitude towards school taken from the home, just as it is hard to "ruin" a child that has been raised with education as a priority. And, largely, homes that are of lower socioeconomic status are typically less likely to have extensive education and are therefore, it appears, less likely to promote education as a priority for their kids. While it would be easy to find specific examples that defy this trend, the overwhelming majority of cases support this.

To remedy this apparent socioeconomic dilemma, the answer is not in the application of the latest and neatest teaching technique. Sometimes groups of teachers have a hard time seeing the larger picture, and begin to promote micro-adjustments to a macro problem. For instance, the latest proposed remedy for closing the socioeconomic academic gap is by "front-loading" vocabulary. "Maybe if we introduce the more difficult words at the beginning of the chapter, we'll even the scores between kids from a certain socioeconomic background and those of the other." Obviously this is incredibly simplistic and doesn't even come close to scratching the surface as to what is going on in society.

For example, if one home limits the hours of t.v. to the minimum, promotes reading, and has discussions at the dinner table about the latest political topic, the child is likely to understand and invest in learning. If another home allows the child to watch endless hours of t.v., doesn't encourage reading, and cusses about how much they hate work at the dinner table, maybe the child won't be as academic. Without even attempting to list the infinite number of variations of the above potential home circumstances, one can immediately see that these influences at home start at birth and have a much larger impact on how a child views the world and his or her place in it. Then, for one hour per day, for nine months or so a year, a teacher tries to introduce a new way of seeing things.

While this "role" of teachers is something that I embrace and continue to do, I am not naive enough to think that a new way of introducing vocabulary or by doing math with colored pens, is going to reverse deep rooted attitudes stemming from one's home-life.

The answer to this situation is likely to come from political and social movements rather than cute new approaches to the same academic subjects. Public policy, like the creation of opportunity for certain socioeconomic regions, a revisit of our standards and who they serve, and an emphasis on creating better parents in our country are closer to being on the scale of change we need to improve academic success for some groups, rather than the continual attempt at finding tiny band aids to cover huge problems.

In the meantime, though, we are fortunate to have teachers that are willing to fight on the front lines, regardless of their odds of success. For any flaws that our teachers have with regards to their classroom policies or their philosophies on success, they have double the positive attributes in the way of caring and passion. Teachers are mostly a good group of people who have a genuine interest in helping kids.

CHAPTER 7: TRACKING

INEVITABLY, WHEN DISCUSSING WHETHER OR not kids are allowed to pursue an individualized path and one that they have passion for, the issue of tracking is brought up. Tracking is the word for the concept of following the direction of your passion or ability, starting at an early age. In the adult world, this notion of specializing in what interests us or is in alignment with what we are naturally good at is seen as what makes our country great.

That is, if we choose to attempt to cure cancer, or if we serve as a fire fighter, we can live an equally full and rewarding life. We make these decisions along the lines of what challenges us and what we consider to be a good use of our time here on this planet. At no point in our existence as Americans are we forced to do a job that we don't want to do, and this is the very essence of freedom and the ability to pursue happiness.

The same concept, when applied to kids in school, has been given the reputation of being restrictive and of closing doors on our kids. The word "tracking," has unfairly taken on a negative connotation. That is, allowing for specialization amongst our kids as early as middle school, and the ability of kids to begin to follow different directions is somehow seen as promoting a caste system or as locking individuals into a life of mediocrity.

For those of you that haven't heard of tracking as it exists in some European nations, it is essentially the idea that along the educational process, at different ages, kids are evaluated for affinity and ability for certain subjects and are moved in one direction or another. That is, if little Suzie aces the math tests, she is allowed, or encouraged, to continue in the direction of math and science, while, little Billy, who doesn't show an ability in the math part, is discouraged from continuing on in math and is led towards a less math intensive career.

In reality, there isn't a division around the world as to whether or not countries employ tracking in their schools, but rather at what age. Even here in the U.S. we have tracking, but it is voluntary and happens at around the age of sixteen. Germany starts tracking at the age of ten, Belgium twelve, Chile fourteen, and Switzerland at the age of fifteen. All of these countries value a comprehensive curriculum for all students, but have determined that a one size box fits all only is applicable up to a certain point, and beyond that, individualization is necessary.

The backlash in this country to tracking seems to be because we feel as though this is un-American. No one can tell our children what they will do for a living twenty years from now, and no one can tell our children that they aren't good at a subject. It is important to remember, though, that we already track our students to a certain degree currently, so the discussion has to be about at what age it should begin.

In the U.S. tracking is imposed by the school and its administrators, but is also self imposed, as kids begin to make decisions about what classes in high school they would like to take. Because of state and federal standards, however, this tracking only happens at the highest levels. For example, if one aims to take calculus, they have to be "signed off" by the teacher of their prior math class. The teacher has to decide whether or not the student has the potential to move on and, of course, the student will have to have had made the choice in the first place that they are up for the challenge. The choice is not there, however, as to whether or not a child takes algebra 1, as it is required to graduate from high school. So, in essence, we as Americans understand and are not put off by tracking to a certain degree, but I would argue that there should be room for self imposed tracking at a younger age.

If one were to look for a model for what that self imposed tracking would look like, our junior colleges provide just that. Celebrated as being extremely successful, our junior colleges offer anything from income producing trades, to simply completing general education classes as a step towards a four year degree. While high school is seen as a waste of time for many of our young, junior colleges are some of the most productive places in our nation.

One can leave a junior college as a dental hygienist, having earned a fire science degree, or a certificate for solar panel installation, and anything in between. The key is that one leaves with an employable skill or the credentials to keep moving forward in education. Currently, for kids who are not likely to move on after high school, they leave high school with nothing. A diploma, aside from being able to read and write, offers no income producing skills.

Notice that junior colleges, while they offer a wide variety of "routes," are not accused of promoting mediocrity or of creating stratification in our society. While a medical assistant, a degree one could attain at a junior college, will earn less than the kid at the junior college that is pre-med, the junior college is seen as simply offering channels for our young to pursue their interests. Community colleges aren't blamed for the discrepancy in outcome between the medical assistant and the doctor, as we as a society recognize that the routes for each individual were a result of internal decisions on the parts of the students themselves. If we were to do this in our high schools, would they be given the same objective critique? Are we so sensitive that we could not make productive changes to our schools so that if a kid so desired, they could attain an employable skill rather than the more abstract type of learning typical for those who intend to go on to a four year school?

But, however, for tracking to make sense in our high schools, it would have to happen on one's own accord, just as is the above case with junior colleges. It is also important to understand that the person wouldn't be tracked in a direction of no value, but rather into something that would be more likely to invoke a passionate response from the kid and thus a potential for success. It serves no one to basically put a kid in house arrest for Algebra 1, only to watch them fail. This does nothing for the kid's self esteem, does nothing for our crowded classrooms, and does nothing for those that actually do want to be in the class.

As for where, specifically, the tracking should begin, I will use math as the example. As I mentioned, algebra 1 and usually geometry are mandatory to graduate from high school, while algebra two and higher are not. Because the incentives are already in place to continue on (college acceptance, social pressure,) I do not think that even algebra 1 and geometry should be mandatory to graduate. I think that all kids should know and understand the arithmetic necessary to existence as an adult, including everything found in a bank or cashier setting, everything pertaining to real estate interactions, calculations of interest on credit card accounts and or savings accounts, and anything else deemed necessary for adult life. For most intents and purposes, this would be up through pre-algebra.

Pre-algebra should be the cut off and the requirement for graduation, and the tracking can begin thereafter. It is almost impossible to make a case that individuals need higher levels of algebra to be successful as adults, as was clearly shown in the chapter of this book titled "curriculum." And to prove the point further, this is where we get the majority of our tutoring business from, as the step from pre-algebra to algebra is when parents begin to not be able to help. There is obviously an issue when we have millionaire parents calling us, stating that the math their kid is doing is over their head.

And, again, this in no way will reduce our competitiveness in the world wide race for scientific achievement, as there is still the huge incentive (wealth) for the kids who desire to go as far as they can in math and science, up until graduation from Stanford or Harvard. Remember, kids do not have to take calculus in high school to graduate, but they still do in relatively large numbers. The difference in no longer making Algebra or Geometry mandatory for high school graduation is that the kids who had no intention of ever going that route in the first place will be spared the useless (to them) information that they fight like bad tasting medicine.

And, if you are worried about the kid who was immature and thus made decisions to limit his or her education, remember the route available to anyone from ages 16 to 99, junior college. We have and will always continue to have this pathway available to any young adult that wishes to start over or to pursue higher learning at any point in their lives. Our junior colleges are wonderful and assure that no choice of direction at an early age will lock a student into a career that they regret.

As it stands now, in a room full of thirty kids taking geometry, only ten want to be there. Ask any teacher or student that you know, if there is a difference between a class of ten kids who sincerely want to be in the class, and a class of thirty who mostly don't. Imagine the difference in education that the ten eager students could receive if the teacher didn't have to worry about fighting the lack of interest with the other twenty. Then consider the classroom management that goes into dealing with the problems that arise from the discontent, and eliminate those. Sounds like utopia doesn't it? Well it would be. The sky is the limit with what those few kids could achieve without the distractions of today's public school ambience.

And to readdress our world competitiveness, it would be much more efficient to hyper educate those who desperately want to and are able to be successful in math and allow the others to find their success elsewhere. And to clarify, that wouldn't mean that the kids who weren't in calculus because they chose not to take it would be out roaming the streets. No, they would be learning how to install solar panels, or how to build computers, or pursuing higher knowledge in our other academic subjects, like literature and history.

Currently, you, as the taxpayer, are paying countless teachers between forty and a hundred thousand dollars a year to teach a subject that has almost no value to kids who have nothing but resentment at the prospect of being given that information. Could the forty to one hundred thousand be paid to teach these kids a skill or a subject that can not only serve them as adults, but excite them about learning? In short, we need to add value to what a high school diploma is. Currently, a high school diploma has little to no income-creating worth.

Someone long ago had the idea right, but from metal shop and wood shop to today, the creativity ran dry. We now have new trades in the world besides making things of metal and wood. Let's take these kids with headaches and a list full of complaints out of "obscure math facts 101" and put them into exciting classes that will literally lead to income and creativity. Just imagine looking at your kids catalog for their high school and seeing the following: solar technology 1, solar technology 2, computer engineering, software engineering, T-shirt printing, landscape design. And yes, in order, you will still see algebra 1 and 2, geometry, and calculus. Essentially, the idea is not new but is rather borrowing from the model that has made our junior colleges so successful.

If we were to alter the standards for graduation and offer more room for individualization in education, I bet enrollment in calculus wouldn't go down in the tiniest bit. Again, kids know that if they want to be competitive in their dream to become engineers from MIT or from Stanford, they'll have to take calculus and do well. Just like we are used to hearing in America, "let the market speak for itself." If no one enrolls in a class, it must have no value.

So, what tracking in essence amounts to is specialization, which to most, is not an unattractive concept. Most of us eventually specialize in a certain field, yet often times the complaint is that we don't find it early enough. It does not take long in the presence of teenagers to see that they are indeed young adults, and many are beginning to plant the seeds of curiosity that will lead them to their own careers and specialties. It is a shame, though, that their investigation has to be independent of school. With what is offered in today's course catalog in public high schools, most have to look to the "real world" for ideas and inspiration. Can we not be more current and offer relevant learning? Could we not replace some of the more technical aspects of math for some of the more practical aspects of life on this planet?

I don't think the task is too daunting to attempt, and this seems to be one of the most fundamental flaws with our secondary school system today. With this rot, a lack of relevance in education, at the base of our secondary schools, small amendments to how our schools are run won't affect much positive change. Without addressing this huge and fundamental issue, we, again, are putting small band aids over huge problems.

CHAPTER 8: WORKLOAD UNFAIR AND MEASUREMENT NOT ACCURATE

INSPIRATION FOR THE TITLE OF this book, and a source of much of the frustration for kids in school, is that how kids are being measured is not accurate. Given all of the factors of the workload for the kid and the minute details of measuring value in our kids, the predicament for many of our kids has become a problem.

From the subjective nature of how many teachers operate, to the process of grading, kids feel swamped and begin to resent the education process. This coupled with the idea that we are expecting our kids to behave less and less like kids, has led to more diagnosis of behavioral disorders and an increasing trend for trying to name what might be causing our kids to struggle. Rather than evaluating the workload or the process of measuring our kids, even though rigor has been increasing year after year, we are more likely to label a kid as apathetic. In the worst case scenarios, we then look to a doctor for solutions as to why the kid isn't performing and seek medical remedies to policy problems.

And even when the case is less extreme, our students are being labeled as average or are being assigned a mediocre letter grade, despite real talent and individuality. With continual feedback of this sort and under such intense micromanagement, it is no wonder that kids report not liking school.

As almost comical examples of how our measurement of kids' value is so far skewed, two stories stand out. One kid, Arturo, is an English language learner, being raised by his mother who only speaks Spanish in the home. He speaks well in English, but Spanish is his primary language. Arturo recently just got a D in Spanish II, from a white teacher from the East coast. The conversation came up as his Spanish teacher cornered me and asked why he was doing well in my class. I responded by asking why he was doing poorly in her class. While I'm sure she can justify the bad grade due to some administrative tasks that he refused to do, his bad grade certainly could not have come from a lack of mastery of the subject. This is what is being referred to in the statement that our kids are being unfairly measured.

In a very similar case, one of my students' lowest grades is in PE despite the fact that she is a star athlete. Even though she wins award after award in three different sports in the county, she has a D- in P.E. It is common sense that she might earn a low grade for a lack of participation, but this doesn't make the situation any less absurd. Do classes exist to serve our kids or do our kids exist to serve the classes? These are some of the factors that contributed to the naming of the book; <u>In Defense of the American Teen.</u>

CHAPTER 9: TEACHERS

A LARGE PART OF THE COMPLAINT from kids is found within the policies of our secondary school teachers and administrators. In every aspect of the job, from grading to classroom management, all teachers are vastly different, but there are some similarities and trends consistent to most teachers. These shared traits likely stem from the school experience that the teachers themselves were raised in, and should probably be revisited to consider whether or not these are positive attitudes.

First off, teachers can be hypocrites. This seems like an exaggeration, but I have found it hard to be amongst such a large group of people that expect something from students, but that speak out so vehemently when they themselves are asked to do a similar task.

The following are some policies that the majority of teachers have that I find absurd, especially when considering their statements at meetings, and in the teacher workroom. First off, it is very common for teachers to complain about work put on them by the administration that doesn't seem to fit into the workday. That is, the number one complaint is that they are expected to do things at home during the evening. Even worse, they might be asked to do things on the weekend as well. They screech that if the action can't happen during the day, when they are being paid, then they shouldn't have to do it.

Naturally, I am in agreement with them. Of course, those extra tasks would cut into well deserved rest, as well as cut into time we would like to dedicate to our loved ones. Many teachers are wonderful family people, placing a huge priority on their kids, and value their time at home. The fact that they moan and groan about having to bring work home is not something that I find repulsive in itself, but rather, that they seem to forget these morals when they sit down to determine the workload for their students.

Most teachers, without pause, agree that it is normal to give at least one hour of homework per night. I can only guess that those same teachers are also under the understanding that they are not the only teacher that the kid has. So they willingly engage in a policy that they blatantly fight for themselves. Doing some quick math, this gives the kids several hours per night of homework. So these teachers can look themselves in the mirror and state they don't want any work to bring home, but have no qualms about sending students home with hours of homework each and every night. Even more appalling is the increasingly common practice of giving work to do over breaks and during the summer vacation. Teachers and teacher unions would never succumb to assignments like these.

While they feel as though their eight or so hours a day are more than enough work for themselves, they don't seem to extend that same sentiment to kids. In addition to the seven or eight hours per day that kids have in school, they are given a few hours of homework per night, bringing their workload to ten or eleven hours a day. Assume that many kids play sports, adding on another couple of hours to their day, and calculate how much free time they have after that.

If you wonder why kids would need free time, again, practice empathy and ask why you wouldn't want a workload of this sort. They need the same well deserved rest, as well as the same time to be with loved ones, as adults do. It wouldn't be hard to argue that they might even need more.

Another issue in which teachers act as hypocrites, that is less important by far, but that adds to the frustration of kids, is that of eating in class. Again, the following isn't a huge crime but is simply a clear act of hypocrisy that I can't get past.

At every teacher meeting, the teachers rustle in their seats and whisper amongst themselves while the speaker addresses the audience, clearly not something that they endorse when they are the figure head in the front of the room. Their opposition to that behavior, though, mysteriously vanishes when the roles are flipped and they are in the students' seats. But a common phrase before a meeting is "at least there is food."

Apparently, time is easier spent and attention is more easily gathered when there is something to snack on. When we go to the movies or sit down for a super bowl, we arrange our snacks well in advance so that they are within reach, while we give our attention to something else. This, by the way is no accident.

Something I remember from my major in molecular, cellular, and developmental biology is that the organ in the human body responsible for consuming the largest amount of glucose (sugar,) we take in, is the brain. It is a metabolically high energy organ, and snacks serve to provide the well needed energy as we push it during things that demand focus. In my tutoring center, I simply won't help a student without snacks and candy readily available on the desk at which we sit.

Anyways, we noble teachers are well aware of this fact, whether by formal education or by simple personal experience, but when it comes to setting policies for kids, as usual, we don't deliver what we demand. The majority of teachers have a strict "no eating" policy in class. They mention that break and lunch are for eating, and that no one will eat in their class. What is appalling, though, about this policy, is found in what they answer upon further probing regarding the rule.

When asked, teachers across the boards have the policy in place, not because it is distracting, but because they don't want crumbs or messes in their room. So, when they sit down and analyze the pros and cons of this, they put aside the likelihood of their kids being tired and mentally down from a lack of glucose, and move in favor of whatever will keep their tidy little room tidy. And furthermore, most administrations support this policy, stating that it is better if everyone enforces the same rules, so there will be less defiance.

So, for the next few teachers meetings, I would like to propose that we eliminate the bagels and tangerines, as well as the juice and coffee, in an attempt to remove the possibility of having a spill or the terrible outcome of a few crumbs on the carpet. Yes, I know that the food helps us to stay alert and is a nice thing to have around to munch on when focusing on a presentation, but too bad, the downsides in the form of a mess are too much to overlook. How do you think they will be with that? They will respond just as the kids have.

Then, in the act of utmost hypocrisy, every teacher in our school designates a week during which time they would willingly reverse the "no eating" policy. During the STAR testing period, in which the school has a serious interest in high scores on this particular exam, the amazing happened. Not only did every teacher, at the instruction of the administration, allow eating during the exam, but the school provided the snacks for the kids directly. That is, each room was given licorice, chips, and chocolates to distribute during the test. As a bribe and a treat, each kid was given snacks.

When I questioned the administration about this, they responded that the food helps the kids to focus and to stay alert, and that they were more likely to do well on the test with snacks. Even though this information was obviously no revelation to me the blatant hypocritical nature of this statement literally caused my eyes to double in size. My next question was obviously, "why wouldn't you want the kids to focus and stay alert on every other single school day of the year?" There was no response.

Because, again, I am a certified teacher and have taught in the classroom, I feel as though I have the authority and the liberty to speak so candidly about teachers. But as I move forward, it is only fair to stress the fact that no two teachers are alike.

It may have been in 1997 or so, when I reached the age of twenty three years old that I realized that there was huge subjectivity in most fields. I was working as a medical assistant for a local clinic and found that certain Physician's Assistants had dramatically different approaches to medicine than others, and that some were simply better. This was so true that we would schedule visits around the ability of different clinicians, and I found the idea disturbing. That is, I felt that if a person wanted to see a doctor, it would be assumed that all doctors are equal in their abilities. After all, when your life is on the line, can you really shop around?

Opinions about everything from which Vitamin Company is better to how to deal with menopause varied from one clinician to the next. While most seasoned adults already understand this idea, it was new to me and painted the world in a slightly different shade of grey. Teachers are no different. From teaching styles and classroom rules and grading, to simple likeability, each teacher is completely different. This fact contributes to the stress of the workload on kids, as well as to the unfair manner in which the kids are measured.

Often new parents will call us for tutoring beginning with the statement that their child has always gotten A's in math and now he has a D. While it may be politically correct to jump to the aid of the teacher in question, the teacher is usually the guilty party. Our tutoring business has, in fact, benefited from the ill work of a few particular teachers in the county, as we have seen a steady flow of new students coming from their math classes. Because these teachers are either unfair or unclear, many otherwise sharp students begin to struggle and soon need our help.

Again, adding to an unreasonable workload and unfair measurement of our kids, many teachers feel as though their classroom is their jurisdiction, and that "while in their room," things will go "my way or the highway." Teachers often employ self made rules that make the challenge of math, or other subjects, unnecessarily more difficult. As I have always assumed that we teach to help kids reach their goals, many policies have left me wondering "how does that help the kid?"

In a discussion with one teacher, the main point of "who do you serve?" came up. I mentioned that I thought that I, as a teacher, served the families of our town. That is, I work to make families and their children in our schools have better and more successful lives. I actually feel as though my policies and my curriculum, while mostly handcuffed to state and federal standards, should address the needs and concerns of my population. I certainly don't feel as though I should lead regardless of what my audience is interested in. But, once I finished with my heartfelt speech, this particular teacher stated " I absolutely don't serve the kids or their families."

When probed, she went on to say that "I serve my subject. I serve the subject of math." Now, to tell you the truth, I'm not even sure what that means, but this is exactly the kind of teacher, detached from reality and his or her role in society, that creates much of the stress that parents and kids today have to deal with. Imagine paying taxes to support a person whose official policy is to not be interested in the specific needs of the kids in their room, but rather to teach minute details of academia and watch the kids either sink or swim.

On top of the volume of work and the subjective nature of school, the fact that many teachers have a tyrannical attitude, is often the final blow for kids. Teachers feel as though they are the kings of their own castles, but they should realize that, just as is the case with our politicians, they are servants to the public.

Unfortunately this trend seems as though it is here to stay, but one movement in particular gives at least a little power back to the people. Where students' only input used to be limited to school ground discussions, they can now use a platform on the internet for discussion as to the effectiveness and appeal of specific teachers. A website called "ratemyteacher.com" has gained popularity and is worth a visit once you put this book down.

The website is organized by city and school, and a person can look up any teacher in any school. The limitation is that the "grades" and comments are added by individuals, so new teachers may not have a full report by the time you investigate them, but older teachers certainly will. The site is run in a classy manner so there are no swear words or baseless attacks on teachers, but the reports are, none the less, candid.

Many people, including myself, might automatically think that a site like this would immediately develop into a public venting site, after a student has been given a bad grade or doesn't like to study, but the kids actually handle themselves in a fair and professional manner. Most of the comments are pretty constructive and a moderator removes much of the slander that would no doubt materialize. Overall, one gets the sense that the site is fair and balanced.

And again, one has to visit the site with the understanding that it is indeed subjective, so some comments might not be representative of the whole population of kids in that teacher's class. As you might imagine, one disgruntled student might be able to taint an otherwise popular teacher, but because of the cumulative nature of the reporting, extreme views are watered down by the masses. Either way, it is at least one way for kids and their parents to hold teachers accountable.

To loosely test the accuracy of the site, some of my tutoring students and I searched for teachers whose reputation we knew well. Overall, the reports were in line with what the word on the street was and teachers that deserved positive reports mostly got them. Similarly, a few of the most despised teachers did in fact show poor ratings and there was even a little space for comments. The comments were of particular value, because the students, presumably, were able to elaborate on their discontent. The site is a start at gaining some sort of accountability from the teachers to the students, but the larger message should be that there is in no way uniformity amongst teachers.

Chapter 10: Homework

THERE IS ONE WORD IN education that can make any person cringe, from age two to ninety two, and that word is homework. The concept of homework is pretty interesting, if one takes a few minutes to analyze its supposed intent and its value, and the topic certainly has earned the honors of having an entire chapter dedicated to it. Homework is often the difference between success and failure for a kid and is definitely, it seems, being overused in schools today. Most parents have a story about how their kid is only in the second grade or so and has a couple of hours of homework per night. Rather than being a sensational story, though, this seems to be the norm in current times.

Before getting too excited or carried away with our personal feelings and personal stories of homework and its ability to consume time that would otherwise be spent as a family unit, it makes sense to take a quick tour of the history of homework in the United States and how we as Americans have viewed it along the way. Attitudes about homework seem to be as subject to change as hair styles, but with much more daunting consequences. It is neat to hear how we as a culture have changed in our attitudes regarding homework and to analyze what historical events helped to shape those changes.

An article printed in the San Francisco Chronicle, in December of 1999, does a fine job of listing key events in the evolution of homework and even legislation passed with it in mind. The article is shown below.

HISTORY OF HOMEWORK
Brian Gill, policy analyst, Rand Corp.; and Steven Schlossman, head of History Department at Carnegie Melon University
Sunday, December 19, 1999

Mid-19th century:
Most students leave school after sixth grade. High school homework is demanding but uncontroversial.

1900-1913:
Ladies' Home Journal takes up a crusade against homework, enlisting doctors and parents who say it damages children's health.

1899-1915:
Various school districts around the country, including San Francisco, Sacramento and Los Angeles, pass anti-homework regulations.

1901:
California legislature passes law abolishing homework in grades K-8, and limiting it in high school.

1948:
National survey shows that median amount of time spent on homework by high school students is three to four hours per week.

1940's-1960's:
Educational debate shifts from abolishing homework to reforming homework and making it more creative and individualized.

1949-1955:
Progressive education movement comes under attack, charged with being anti-intellectual and insufficiently rigorous. Pro-homework movement forms.

1957:
Launch of Sputnik gives pro-homework movement a boost, setting off concerns that American students aren't keeping up with Russian counterparts.

1983:

"A Nation At Risk" denounces "rising tide of mediocrity" in American schools. Three years later, the U.S. Department of Education publishes pamphlet called "What Works" and concludes that homework does.

1990s:
Overwhelming consensus in favor of homework: among both educators and general public. Many districts have policies requiring homework. Survey shows level of high school homework hasn't increased, but amount given to kids in elementary school has gone up dramatically.

From the above, I found a few things interesting. First, because of my natural tendencies to find homework to be an assault on what childhood stands for, I was thrilled to see an actual piece of legislation prohibiting homework for kids less than fifteen years of age. And while this doesn't address the kids that I primarily teach, who are in middle and high school, it certainly sets the tone for an overall judgment on homework, and had acted as a beacon of light for all teachers in high school not to abuse homework as a policy.

What also stands out to me is that we moved towards homework out of fear, rather than productive thought and creative discussion on the topic. The launch of the Sputnik, by the Russians, as the article stated, created anxiety in America about whether or not we were competitive in math and science. At any cost, people seemed to cling to anything that might have given us an edge over the Russians during the famed "Cold War," regardless of whether or not it was healthy for our young.

Maybe now is a good time to point out some other brilliant policies that stemmed from our fear of communism, like the red scare. Probably never in the history of mankind have the best ideas come from a place of fear and intimidation, bur rather from free minds that are set on coming up with a solution in which the best interests of all are considered.

What I also find interesting is how we are constantly acting to remedy the apparent problem underlying the statistics regarding our supposed lack of dominance on the world scene. As an average, we score below Korea or other nations, and the next politician swears to turn things around. Without much deep thought, it seems easy to point out the lack of logic in this line of reasoning.

The average doesn't matter. If we have a thousand top minds that outscore Korea in innovation, we have the advantage. If we have the capital to recruit from the top scoring nations, we have the advantage. And frankly, being the largest melting pot in the world, we have social problems to deal with that will certainly throw our averages off, but that won't slow us down as a nation. Because of our diversity, this is the greatest nation in the world, but it might not serve our bottom line on test scores. This is a country in which a musician, a politician, a craftsman, and a scientist can all be successful. Should we sacrifice that so we have a few points higher of an average on our overall math scores?

And while our kids were being deemed less than average, did we not rock the world with the largest technological boom of the last few generations with the advent of computing and software? Driven by primarily American companies, the advances made during the nineties were awesome in their size and ability to change the daily lives of millions. Let's not forget that these technological advances were masterminded by our so called less than average citizens.

And frankly, the average citizen in America still isn't able to create an ascetically pleasing computing machine that runs on software, uses some technical coding system, and that is able to allow a person to email, watch movies, and do banking online. To maintain our lead in technology, should we add this to our high school curriculum? Obviously every soul in America doesn't have to be an expert in calculus for us to succeed in the sciences and in math. Thus, an increase in homework to boost a mundane score, like our average in math and science, seems like a fruitless task.

And finally, an era that is arguably responsible for some of our greatest social movements and our most uninhibited thinking, the sixties and just before, had a policy that might just be the perfect middle ground for both the anti homework and homework loving camps. The policy, as stated in the article, was a movement towards being more creative and individualized with the use of homework. This seems to hit the nail on the head.

There can certainly be a case made for room for learning at home, and especially for projects that take real world experiences or things that are more time consuming than the school schedule will allow. But again, if one were to consider homework on these terms, the assignments would certainly have to be creative and individualized.

I have long argued for homework that is project based and student driven. That is, rather than route memorization or tedious worksheets, the home is a place for projects that may take months to mature and that would likely involve parental support. As an example, I would support homework for Physics class that was to build a structure over the duration of the semester that could float and support X amount of weight. This would certainly qualify as being creative and individualized, as the student him or herself would be involved in designing the project.

While I certainly do not assign nightly homework to my math classes, as I recognize they are skew from the point of learning and creative growth, I do have a fourth quarter project that the kids are to do at home. Rather than having the tone of a boring set of problems that are due the following day, the fact that the project is being done away from the classroom is often secondary to what the project is and how the kids will put it together.

Each student has to pick a career of their choice, thus bringing in individualism, and construct a comparison of how a person with that career would do in four cities around the United States. The comparison is entirely financial, bringing in math concepts that apply to real life, and is a lesson for the kids relating to real choices that they will have to make as they become young adults. For example, if a students mentions that they would like to be a teacher, they are to research teachers incomes against the expenses of life in the cities of their choice. They might choose New York, San Francisco, New Orleans, and Omaha. The choice, again, is theirs but I suggest to them that they look for drastically different places to make the point more clear.

Then, they have to analyze the cost of living in those cities. They are to investigate the average cost of rent or a mortgage, along with the cost of groceries, utilities, and other practical expenses associated with living. Finally, bringing all of the numbers together, they have to present to the class, in the form of a power point, how different their lives would be in these different places as a teacher. Could they afford to live in New York? Would it be in a house or a tiny apartment? Could they buy a home in Omaha? Would one income be enough to live in San Francisco? For once, the math assignment is something that we as adults actually deal with in real life, and therefore automatically has more value for the kids, whether they are conscious of this fact or not. But, because the project is time consuming, it makes sense to assign it over a long period, and to have the kids do it at home.

Because the above article regarding homework ends at 1999, a question might be as to how things are shaping up today. While we are well aware of our sentiments in the local schools around us, national data is helpful to see where we are heading as a country. A more recent article, taken from the internet on 12/2/09, (http://social.jrank.org/pages/992/Trends-in-Elementary-Secondary-Education) had the following to say.

Trends in Elementary and Secondary Education - Why So Much Homework?

"The media report that in the race to keep up with the world's highest academic achievers, kids are overloaded with homework and are in danger of burning out," the article states.

The article then goes on to display statistics showing that teachers are assigning a little more homework, but students aren't spending any more time doing it. There was little change in the amount of time students reported spending on homework.

The article goes on "In 1999, more 13-and 17-year-olds were skipping homework. Fewer spent time on it when they did do it. NCES reports that in 1999 more than half of all students spent less than five hours a week to homework."

"Does it make any difference how much time children spend on homework? NCES says: 'Homework may have a positive effect on older students' achievement, but no discernible effect on the achievement of younger students.' Professor Harris Cooper of the University of Missouri, Columbia, who has researched the homework question, claims there is a 15-year cycle to the homework issue. Every 15 years there is a call to abolish it, followed 15 years later by a call for more of it.

American 4th-graders scored above average in math and near the top in science. American 8th-graders were about average in both. By 12th grade, American students scored below the international average and ranked nearly at the bottom. Newspaper headlines called the American scores "dismal" and American performance 'mediocre.'"

To comment on the last article, I found a piece of information to be particularly interesting and it has been the basis for my disinterest in homework for awhile now. Regardless of what we want from homework, we have to ask ourselves if it is working. We shouldn't only ask the philosophical questions about the potential gains or losses from homework, but should look for some "on the ground" results. In many discussions with other teachers I have expressed the concern that, like it or not, homework isn't working.

Kids often just don't do their homework and when they do, it is with such little passion that the alleged gains are lost. What would be ideal is that when kids did sit down to learn, it was with all of their focus. If we give our kids too much to do, they will begin to do a more and more poor job. The article addressed this exact issue.

The article mentioned how kids would simply not do the extra homework assigned, as I have certainly seen in school and as a tutor, and if they do the work, it is with the sole interest of completing the bare minimum to get by. Was this the intent of the founders of homework? And frankly, I find it hard to blame a kid at the age of fourteen for being tempted to throw in the towel when the workload becomes too much. The life of the focused student becomes so unattractive that they are more willing to adopt the role of a mess-up, and shun the system.

Then, another huge issue with regards to homework that is less reported on, and is a harder issue to nail down an accurate statistic for, is that of kids cheating on homework. In the case of long dry homework assignments, like the 1-55 odd in math, or the three page fill in the blank worksheets for Spanish, a huge percentage of kids simply "get it at break." That is, students regularly count on a few kids to complete the work, and then in five minutes during lunch or break, they simply copy the assignment in its entirety. Because I am a tutor and one that the majority of the kids confide in, I have heard the above countless times…"I'll just get it at break."

Recall, this is not an attempt to report kids and to list the reasons that our kids are failures, but rather to point out that the current system in place for homework in most classes isn't working. If otherwise great kids feel the need to cheat on a daily basis to maintain a certain grade, we may want to reevaluate the demands we have placed on them. It is possible that every kid in America isn't a lazy bum, but that as things stand now, school has a surreal and almost bizarre tone to it. 1-55 odd in every class, every night, is simply ridiculous.

At a local high school, one math teacher mentioned that he gave only one hour of homework per night, which, he went on, is not that much. It should be noted that one hour is a conservative guess, as the kids that struggle with the subject are likely going to toil over the assignment for well over an hour. But what this teacher fails to remember is that the kid has five other classes. To give a real life math problem, "how much homework does a kid have per night if each teacher, from a schedule of six classes, gives just one teeny tiny hour of homework per night?"

And for the counter argument that many classes, like P.E. and art don't give homework, even that is changing. PE is giving homework now. One of my students brought his PE homework to my office and we had to memorize the muscles and bones of the human body. And while this seems useful, could it not be done in class? Every subject in every school from the second grade on seems to find it necessary to send more tasks home. This trend is leaving the territory of being just a bummer, and is entering the realm of becoming a national crisis. We are fundamentally redefining childhood and the changes, I would argue, are not for the better.

If you were to spend a few minutes on the philosophy behind homework, you'd find that there is only a place for it in a limited setting. For instance, it doesn't make sense to expect a student to do homework in math for material they haven't learned. That is, if the material is new and their parents didn't graduate from Berkeley with math degrees, the assignment will only be a huge lesson in frustration. So often, teachers give assignments as a precursor to what they'll discuss in class the following day, but this, for math in particular, is a recipe for disaster. For complex subjects, the majority of the kids are unable to navigate the material in a productive way and only develop a defeatist attitude about the course. The same is true if something has only been discussed briefly and it is assumed that the kid will do his or her own research to find solutions.

Then, if the homework is given as a tedious set of hoops to jump through, it is nothing but a waste of time. I, as a tutor, can always tell when assignments had little thought put into them when teachers say "do 1-55 odd." Did they look at all of those and determine that they are key problems that will really drive home the point, or did they feel as though they had to fulfill their responsibility to dole out assignments each night to keep from turning heads.

Then, more often than not, it would be too time consuming to correct each kid's five hundred problems per night, so the teacher gives the kid a plus or a check or a stamp for writing some work down. If a kid gets them all wrong, receives his or her check/plus, and never is offered an explanation to how the problems should have been done, how is this anything but a disservice to the kid?

Then, what is even worse is if the homework is graded for accuracy. Grading homework for accuracy is akin to a take home test and clearly favors the kids with tutors or parents with backgrounds in math. In a situation like this, a kid who sits down for two hours to complete the assignment could be given an F for their efforts. This is the quickest way to ensure that kids will cheat to get by. In fact, if a system is this unfair, it actually only makes sense to copy someone else's answers. It certainly doesn't make sense to struggle every night for two hours, with no help, to be given an F on every assignment. This is just ridiculous.

The following is an example of exactly what I'm talking about. To protect the ridiculous and innocent alike, no names will be mentioned, but rest assured that both the teacher and student are real, living, and breathing human beings. The latter has a big heart and is trying to succeed, while the former has an actual piece of cold steel where the heart would be supposed to be present. Okay, that was a slight exaggeration, but look at the work below and you'll understand. And as you might have imagined, I will be making a few constructive comments after the work has been reviewed by you.

In particular, pay attention to the work and its organization. Ask yourself if it looks as though the student rushed through the work and blew the assignment off, or if the student dedicated over an hour and a half of their night to the assignment. Also, ask yourself if you would have been able to help this kid during their work and your answer will likely be the answer that her actual parents had.

She did this alone, at home, without the presence of a tutor or a parent that majored in math. This being so, ask yourself if there is anything above and beyond what she did that she possibly could do. Okay, enough said. Enjoy.

Assignment evens
Practice A

$3/a$

class 1   84

Q $-3 = 5 - 2d$
$-5 \quad -5$
$-8 = 2d$
$\frac{}{2} \quad \frac{}{2}$
$-4 = d$

④ $-13 = 52y$
$\frac{}{52} \quad \frac{}{52}$
$-4 = y$

⑥ $0.21p = 2.42 - p$
$-2.42 \quad -2.42$
$\frac{2.63p}{2.63} = \frac{-p}{2.63}$
$p = -2.63$

⑧ $3(6t-2) - 8 = 5 - t$
$3(6t-2) - 8 = 5 - t$
$3(6t) - 3(2) - 8 = 5 - t$
$9t - 6 - 8 = 5 - t$
$\quad -2 \qquad -2$
$9t \qquad = 3 - t$
$+t \qquad \quad +t$
$\frac{10t}{10} \qquad = \frac{3}{10}$
$\qquad t = \frac{3}{10}$

⑩ $5s - 7 \leq 12, (4)$
$5(4) - 7 \leq 12$
$20 - 7 \leq 12$
$13 \not\leq 12$

⑫ $12 - (4 - x) > 0 \qquad (-8)\ 12 - (4-x) > 0$
$12 - (4 - 8) > 0 \qquad 12 - (4(7)) > 0$
$12 - 12 > 0 \qquad\quad 12 - 12 \ 0 \quad 0$
$\quad 0 \not> 0 \qquad\qquad\quad 0 \neq 0$

⑭ $2.5k + 3 \geq 4.5$
$\qquad -3 \quad\ -3$
$\frac{2.5K}{2.5} \quad \frac{1.5}{2.5}$
$\boxed{K \geq .6}$
✓ use fraction

⑯
$-20 \geq 11y + 13$
$-13 \qquad\quad -13$
$\frac{-33}{11} \quad \frac{11y}{11}$
$\boxed{-3 \geq y}$ ✓

⑱ $\frac{4h}{-5} - 4 \geq 16$
$\qquad\quad +4 \quad +4$
$\frac{-5}{4} \cdot \frac{4h}{-5} \geq 18 \frac{-5}{4}$
$h \leq -95/2 \quad \boxed{h \leq -25}$

$\frac{4h}{-5} - 4 \geq 16$
$\frac{4h}{-5} \geq 20$
$4h \leq -100$
$h \leq -25$

⑳ $4(-2)^2 + b > 36$
$4(+4) + b > 36$
$16 + b > 36$
$-16 \qquad -16$
$\qquad b > 20$

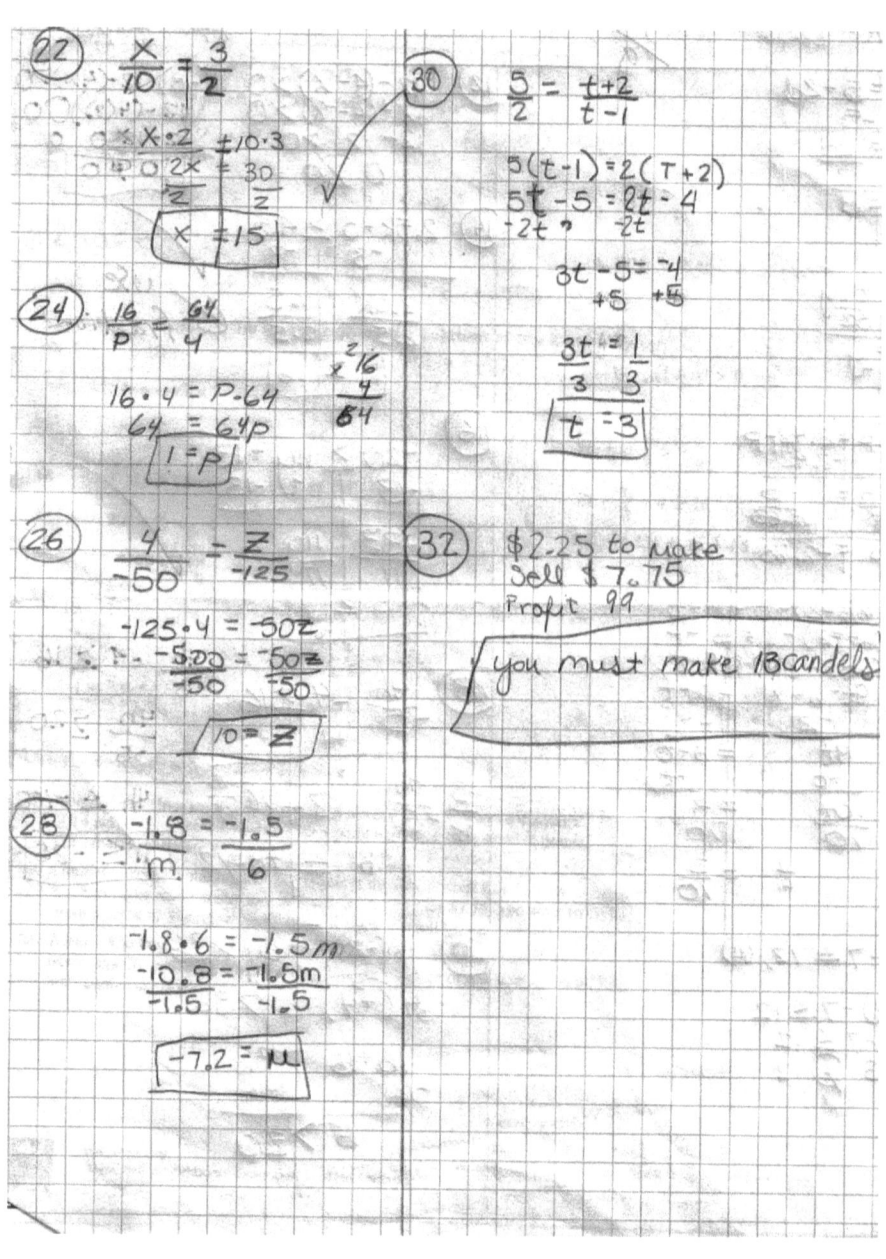

22 $\dfrac{x}{10} = \dfrac{3}{2}$

$x \cdot 2 = 10 \cdot 3$

$\dfrac{2x}{2} = \dfrac{30}{2}$

$\boxed{x = 15}$

24 $\dfrac{16}{P} = \dfrac{64}{4}$

$16 \cdot 4 = P \cdot 64$

$\dfrac{64}{64} = \dfrac{64p}{64}$

$\boxed{1 = P}$

$\dfrac{^2 16}{4} = 64$

26 $\dfrac{4}{-50} = \dfrac{z}{-125}$

$-125 \cdot 4 = -50z$

$\dfrac{-500}{-50} = \dfrac{-50z}{-50}$

$\boxed{10 = z}$

28 $\dfrac{-1.8}{m} = \dfrac{-1.5}{6}$

$-1.8 \cdot 6 = -1.5m$

$\dfrac{-10.8}{-1.5} = \dfrac{-1.5m}{-1.5}$

$\boxed{-7.2 = m}$

30 $\dfrac{5}{2} = \dfrac{t+2}{t-1}$

$5(t-1) = 2(T+2)$

$5t - 5 = 2t + 4$

$-2t \qquad -2t$

$3t - 5 = -4$

$+5 \qquad +5$

$\dfrac{3t}{3} = \dfrac{1}{3}$

$\boxed{t = 3}$

32 $2.25 to make
Sell $7.75
Profit 99

you must make 13 candels

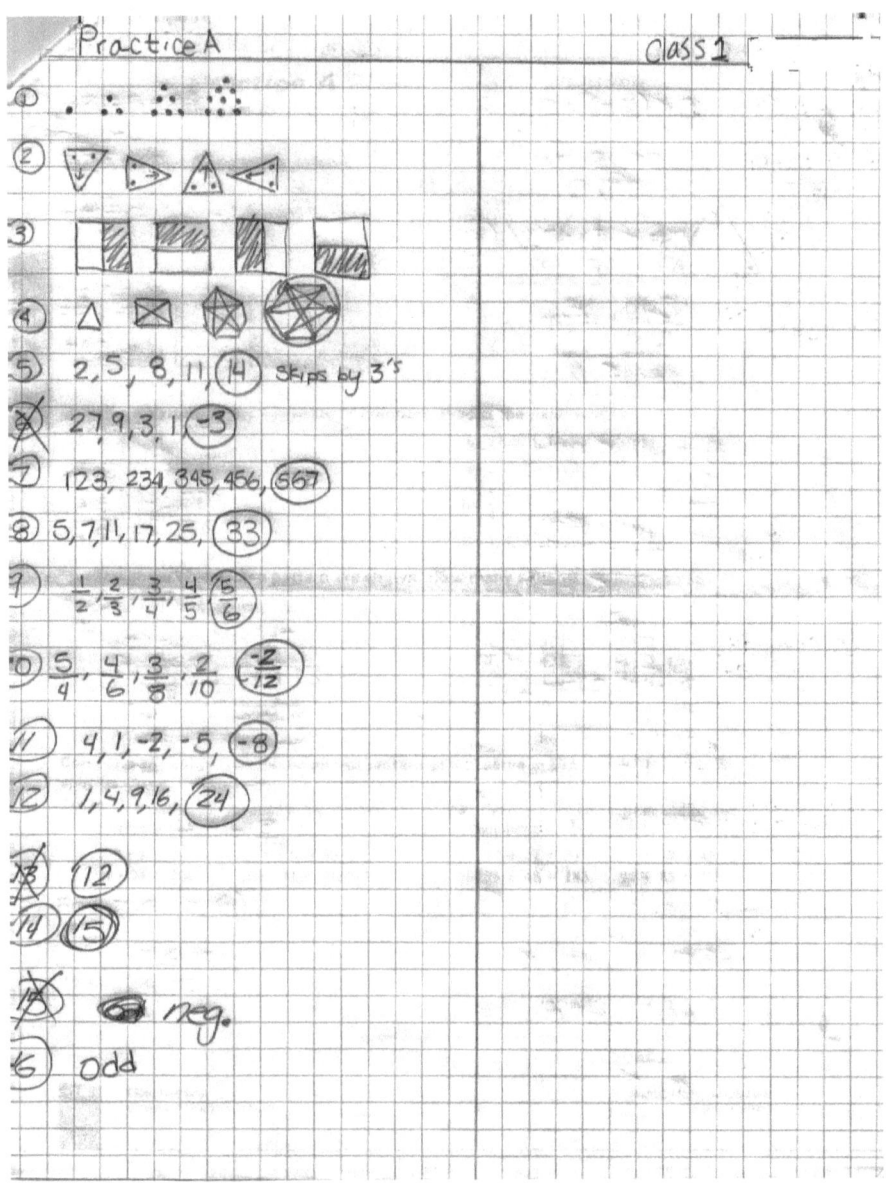

Okay, now that we have taken that little aside, what did you think? If you are thinking that wrong is wrong and a kid shouldn't get credit for wrong answers, it seems as though you are referring to tests. So basically, this teacher has set up a situation in which a kid has tests in class and a test every single night for homework.

Also, did you notice that the teacher assigned evens, so the kid can't check her answers in the back of the book. The reason they have answers in the back of the book is because there is nothing more frustrating than doing a math problem at home and not knowing if it is even right or wrong. Because the teacher wanted to prevent cheating, he created a situation where kids do fifty problems per night and don't know that they did them all wrong until the following day, when they receive their F. So, as expected, this kid got them wrong, received an F and was never truly shown how to correct her work. And actually, an F is 50% and this teacher gave this girl a 33%, which is much lower than an F.

So let's review, for all of her hard work at home, she was given a 33%, well below an F, only to go to class and pick up her next assignment for the coming night. Sounds like a great model for learning. Now, can someone explain to me why the best thing to do is to keep trying and not to get the answers from her friend? This is why cheating is rampant amongst kids with homework assignments. Kids in this particular class cheat because this teacher has set up a certain failure situation.

And maybe the most important thing to take away from this is how to accept news from your own kid about a bad grade. If the parents of this girl were not involved, and didn't understand, they might have simply looked at the grade and scolded her for such poor results. Surely an F would necessitate some sort of punishment from the parents. But the opposite is actually true.

More often than not, kids need an advocate more than someone on their case about grades. Grading is the must subjective thing in the world and don't be quick to yell at your kid for a score alone. Do the due diligence and get on their case only after that is done. A lot of times, it is the teacher that deserves the scathing lecture.

This teacher does indeed exist and fails an exceptionally high number of kids, which means either he is a lousy teacher or that he grades too hard. But, because of the T word, (tenure,) kids will be writing his name on bathroom walls for years to come.

If however, the teacher does spend time doing the problems in class, the question becomes, "why couldn't they have skipped the homework and done the problems in class to begin with?" The way it should be done is that small sets of problems should be done in class and the kids should get instant feedback after no more than a few problems or less. This is how learning is best achieved in math. It doesn't make sense to do an entire math assignment wrong, only to go on to try to unlearn the bad habits the following day in class.

Homework should not be considered a default or a mandatory bureaucratic part of school. Teachers shouldn't go through teaching programs assuming that they will have to shoulder the burden of "coming up" with some assignment on a daily basis to keep the status quo. Homework had better have a very real purpose or should be eliminated entirely.

The situations in which homework is useful and does make sense, is when the task simply can't be done within the walls of the classroom. For instance, I would support a homework assignment in which students were asked to go out into society and interview professionals on a particular subject. I would also support a homework assignment in which kids were asked to visit a local animal shelter and conduct some sort of statistical analysis of the number of animals abandoned, and or adopted each month. These assignments are of value, but can't be done in a school day, and as a secondary perk, these types of assignments often involve the help of parents and family and can be fun as well as educational. There are many valuable lessons that simply can't be learned within the boundaries of a small classroom, but problems "1-55 odd" isn't one of them. These are academic reasons for why homework isn't working.

Besides the academic reasons for arguing against such tedious and excessive homework, a philosophical argument against homework and its effect on the standard of living of our kids is just as important. The majority of my concerns with homework have to do with my love for family and the value I place on loved ones. The importance of family and time with siblings and parents might be the number one reason I have waged this war against excessive homework.

What a romantic picture to imagine a kid coming home from high school only to pal around with family, both fighting and laughing, but being together. After school and work, wouldn't it be neat to see everyone telling funny stories about the day's twists and turns. Maybe the moment could come up about how to deal with a jealous kid in class or about how to avoid getting into fist fights with bullies. Maybe they could watch a favorite t.v. show together. Maybe they could sit down to have dinner, even if it involved complaints about broccoli and snide comments about one another. Then, even if the stresses of each day cause more tension than release, there will be the inevitable moment or moments when the whole family laughs together and everyone feels a sense of belonging. After all, we are all going to have enough of not seeing each other when the kids are old enough to move out, who wants extra "not seeing each other" now.

Having the teenager retire to the den or bedroom to frantically keep up with the "1-1000 odd" assignment is not romantic and is bordering on sad. For kids that play sports and hope to maintain a decent G.P.A., the above scenario is a reality, and because the majority of the readers of this book are parents, I don't have to argue the case. You have likely lived firsthand seeing your child locked away in their room in an attempt to simply do the bare minimum.

More and more kids are having, rather than an upbringing full of discussions with family, a childhood where family time has been replaced by "1-55 odd" and countless book reviews. Academics are certainly important, but are they more important than family? I personally think that more can be learned from hearing one another talk about life, work, and daily issues, than from a math book.

Recently, during an open house meeting in which parents visited my class, a parent asked in a skeptical tone about my policy of not having homework for my high school geometry class. Naturally, he was concerned, as his own experience with both his education and that of his teenager included homework as the standard. Being different, the policy of no homework made him nervous, in fear that his child might fall behind. At the end of the day all parent actions, rational or not, have the best of intentions for the well being of their kid. I found this concern to be natural.

In answering, though, I stated that a kid should absolutely be learning at home. Kids should learn at home, but in lieu of fractions, maybe the kid might learn something from discussions with his mom and dad. Maybe they could replace the two hours of math with two hours of discussing how their days went. Maybe they could talk about not smoking cigarettes or how to deal with girlfriends and or boyfriends. Maybe the parents could explain the ins and outs of their jobs and adult life to their kids. Can we as parents really not find a topic to discuss at home without hours of tedious academia to replace what used to be the passing on of family values and stories? I obviously have an opinion as to which would be a better use of time, but others seem more reluctant to follow.

Once the parents headed for the door, though, one mother asked to speak with me and stated that I had "given her daughter back" to her. Literally holding back tears, she explained that in the last few years, she rarely had time to spend with her child. She went on to thank me and she said she wished other teachers understood.

Her daughter is an excellent student, and to maintain her outstanding grades, she was required to be absent for most of the night. Because math is often times the subject that is most guilty of abusing homework, having no math at night gave them more time to just be together. If I accomplish nothing else this year, giving this mom more time with her little girl is something I can hang my hat on.

In my math classes at a local public high school, we do the same amount of actual problems as happens in the more traditional classes, but the work is done on my watch. That is, because the kids are in class and not doing the work at home, if they get stuck they can simply ask a peer sitting next to them for assistance or for my help directly. The frustration of doing ten problems in a row incorrectly, only to wait for twenty fours hours to find that out, is removed. Also, I as a teacher can get a better sense of how the group is doing as a whole and can redirect activities on the spot if needed. The constant support that the kids receive, coupled with my constant supervision of their progress makes work in class much more productive than work at home would be.

And upon having this discussion of the value of homework with my sharper students from my geometry class, I decided to give a voice to students that we so often debate about. I told all of them to write down a few sentences as to what they don't like about homework, on a half sheet of paper. If we are truly interested in finding the best way to educate these kids, a few minutes dedicated to hearing their thoughts could only be productive, and below are some of their comments.

Originally, I figured that the kids and their opinions would be discounted, as most of us adults assume that all teenagers will take the easiest route possible, and having no homework qualifies as the easiest route in this case. And while I still think this is largely true, they bring up some points that I had neglected to mention. Overall, our kids are really awesome and they deserve a second on the podium; so kids, here is your shot at the big leagues.

To record history accurately, though, I'll admit that I hand picked which responses to include, and left out comments like "man... homework sucks... man," even though that was a class favorite. I only encouraged eloquent thought on the subject. The kids just jotted down their immediate thoughts, with little preparation or attention to grammar and such. I liked a few of them.

To drive home the point that this feedback was coming from some of my elite students, I had them write down their GPA, anticipating the counter argument that the following is not the attitude of the college bound groups. It certainly is. Here goes.

The first letter was in response to my question as to how many kids just copy the "1 through 55" homework during the lunch before the period. Most answered ranged from 60 to 90 percent, so I had this kid just throw down his average response.

70% of people copy math homework at lunch

Whether we like it or not, this figure seems to be pretty accurate. Whether or not the cheating is justified or is in direct response to the absurdity of the assignments or not, one has to question the value in something that only 30% of kids are doing. One teacher responded by saying "yeah, well that gets sorted out during tests." This may be true, but it makes the assignments no less productive, but only ensures revenge on the part of the teacher.

The next letter came from a girl who's parents both live in Mexico and don't speak English. She lives with her Aunt who speaks some broken English and is very supportive, but not well off financially. I know this detail because I talked to her and her aunt, and this student is the twinkle of her family's eye. Just note the GPA and the sweet attitude and you'll know why they adore her. This letter at first seems like a low down attempt from me to get you where you are softest, a little girl doing chores along with her school work to get by, but is absolutely a real situation. This kid is doing great, but is a servant to a weird scenario.

> GPA : 4.0
>
> I'm a Senior and I only sleep 6 hours because when... I need to do my homework from all my classes. When I arrived at home I need to help in home by cleaning and cooking. Then I set down and do my homework all the rest of the day until 12 or 1 of the morning. Then during class time I'm sleepy and can't concentrate because of all the time I did not sleep.

This girl just recently announced to me that she had won a scholarship for five thousand dollars to attend the local junior college after high school. Once you've dried your eyes and are ready to move on, just give me a nod. Okay, next letter.

This one is from my "prima donna," amazing, soon to be a doctor or a lawyer student. This kid is from a very academic family and is shocking in both his work ethic and natural ability.

I especially valued his response because I actually thought that if anyone would defend homework, it would be this kid. To my surprise, he wrote the following. And although the GPA written on the notes could obviously be fabricated, you are just going to have to take my word for it. Anyways, read away.

Homework is just excersise, not learning. If you understand it,
it's pointless. If you don't understand it, you can't do it
and you still don't learn anything.
                    GPA from last year   4.167

The next letter might be the most frustrating of all. Originally, homework was created to supplement a kid's learning, but has now become an animal of its own. If one understands the material, homework shouldn't be employed right? Or if it is, should it be optional?

I spoke to this mom, before her son was transferred to my class, and she was beside herself. She couldn't believe that a situation so absurd had come up and that the teacher could be so "expletive here" to not see the insanity in her policy. Her son was getting B's on all of his tests, but because he wasn't doing homework, his grade was brought down to an F and he didn't pass. Let me repeat, he knew eighty percent of the math and was given a failing grade.

last year I got B's on the test and failed because I didnt do my homework and when I did my Homework I'd only get 5 or 6 out of 10.

Marshall

And for the record, and to paint a clear picture, this kid is no lazy bum by any means. He is what we as adults respect, but is not rewarded in high school for his character. He is a three sport athlete, does well in school, and is one of the most sociable kids in my class. When you picture a good wholesome kid with an eye on what counts, this kid comes up. He certainly didn't prioritize sniveling over a few points for homework and, in the case of his last teacher, was punished for being well rounded and not playing the game. In my class this kid has an A and is a complete pleasure to have in the room. It is a crime to have labeled him as a failure the year before.

So, as we discuss and analyze what is and isn't working in our secondary schools, homework has to be given a long and critical look. Is homework serving our kids, or are our kids serving homework?

CHAPTER 11: GRADING

So along the lines of our kids being measured unfairly and the demands on kids becoming ridiculous, what about grading? To question something that is so common place that we accept it without much thought at all, grades are one of the most bizarre and interesting things in school today. That is, if we started the whole field of education from scratch today, would we place grades as such a high priority that it would dominate nearly every discussion between teacher and parent?

If one were to spend a great deal of time contemplating the nature of grades, the inevitable conclusion would be that grades have absolutely no value in learning, but serve only as an administrative tool for schools and universities to have a basis for selecting students. Really, there can be nothing productive about grading someone if your aim is to teach them a skill or ability.

For instance, I have spent the last few days teaching my four year old little girl how to ride a bike, with both "hands on" training and miniature lectures in which I tell her where to place her hands and how to brake. While I consider her learning of the lesson of how to ride a bike to be of the utmost importance, at no time did I consider that giving her a grade might somehow help me to reach this goal.

And for a more academic example, I place a huge value on reading and the power of novels and non-fiction books to increase our vocabulary and their ability to enhance our general knowledge about the world around us. I will demand that my girls be readers throughout their young and adult lives and have already spent time thinking about how I will make it fun for them. At no point, though, have I stopped to think about how I might grade their progress. A letter grade or a grade in any other form is absolutely of no use to me or my girls as it pertains to their growth as readers. In fact, grades could only bring a negative element into the scenario, creating angst and a sense of being micro-managed. This would kill the spirit to read and to enjoy great literature. Yet, grades are a center piece in education today.

The funny thing is that most parents of the kids that I tutor will say that they don't care about grades. They understand the idea that grades shouldn't be the central goal, but can't escape from the fact that good grades are like wealth in a way. Just as we feel proud in a newer car and often flaunt our financial success, good grades are brought up readily at cocktail hour with a sense of pride, and are even paraded around town on bumpers to show our achievements. I have never seen a bumper sticker that said "my kid is learning a lot and becoming a well-read and well-rounded person." No, it is absolutely the results that we want from our kids and most families, today, use this as a measure of success.

The parents who state that grades aren't important to them always say the same thing. Without exaggeration, I have heard the exact same line from multiple families. They often say "we don't care about grades, we just ask for B's." Do you see the irony in that statement? They say they don't care about grades and then deliver an exact grade related goal that they deem acceptable. If your goal for your child is to have A's, or even C's, as is the case for many of my kids, you have a grade oriented goal.

For the kids that I tutor, I really have only one goal for my students, and that is that they become successful as young adults. If grades are the route to success, then so be it. If grades aren't the route to success for that particular kid, though, it is time to start thinking of all options. In no way is the only route to success through the traditional path of good grades in school and then career. Look at the founders of Apple and Microsoft, if you'd like an example of "outside of the box" thinking. There are countless success stories that pivot around following one's passion before following an empty goal like a letter grade.

I have almost never had a parent call me and ask for help with tutoring so that their child may learn more or that they may be inspired to learn, but rather that they need help in getting their grade up. This "getting their grade up," is common slang amongst parents. I don't judge them, though, in the least, as it is true that grades to a certain degree can certainly limit opportunity or open more doors. This is stressful for parents and kids alike, but by analyzing what they even mean, it is possible to reduce some of that stress.

The University of California, Santa Cruz, where I earned my B.A. in molecular, cellular, and developmental biology, had the right idea and was one of the only universities in America to offer evaluations in place of grades. We were not given letter grades, no matter our major, but were given actual narratives instead. But, as is often the case with fresh new ideas, the evaluations were pushed aside to make room for letter grades the year I graduated. It turned out, as is the case with high school students as well, that the evaluations were proving too difficult to translate for graduate programs. PhD programs, medical schools, and so on, were having a hard time judging the applicant in an objective way with evaluations and were requesting that old transcripts be translated into letter grades. When I applied to medical school, my transcripts underwent the same conversion, and my narrative comments were switched to actual letter grades. UCSC undertook an interesting experiment that was eventually proven to be too cumbersome for our American way. Grades are here to stay.

The huge misconception, though, is that grades are an objective tool by which to measure kids' success and effort. Very few things in this world are less objective than grades and grading policies, with almost no uniformity from teacher to teacher, let alone school to school, or district to district.

To give you a rough idea as to what I mean, every teacher places different weights on tests versus other assignments, while some don't even share the same categories. Some teachers do group tests, some do take home tests. Some teachers allow notes for tests, while some do not. Some teachers allow kids to recover points by doing test corrections, while some do not. Some teachers grade homework literally, while some do the "check" mechanism. Some classes are just flat out easier than others, but are worth the same credit as their counterparts. Some districts in their entirety are easier, while some are more demanding, but the grades go to the same place.

There are home-schooled kids who have virtually all A's with no tests, while other kids attend rigorous private schools and struggle to maintain B's. Some kids have tutor support with their take-home work or help from parents, while others struggle alone. Summer school courses are only six weeks long but count as much as a whole year course, and are traditionally much easier. The list of discrepancies goes on and on, yet grading is allegedly an objective process. Do not be confused, grading is not objective at all.

Yet, again, it appears that there is no other way for bureaucracies to process student applications, and so we move on in that direction. The only objective tool for universities, but a tool with its own flaws, is the SAT.

To further distort our kids' actions from the true meaning of school and learning is the concept of cramming for the SAT and other standardized tests. Originally these tests were designed to be a snapshot of what a kid does or doesn't know at a certain point in their lives. Then, as should have been predicted, kids began to cram for these tests and scores rose. Shortly thereafter there came the advent of SAT prep courses and books, with the sole aim of raising scores so that kids could be accepted to their school of choice. At no time did the founders of these prep materials have an interest in developing passion for the subjects on the test or for true depth of knowledge, but, just as advertised, were designed to increase your score by X amount. This is a classic case of "teaching to the test."

Now, as scores on average increase, the demands on our kids increase as well. Not only do they have too much homework and too dry of classes, they are expected to outscore their counterparts by cramming with weekend programs and by burning through books several inches high. The system has spun out of control and the true meaning of "learning" has been lost.

I can imagine a steel-smith passing his trade onto his son, or a business owner in today's world training her daughter to take over the reigns. In these above cases, the focus of every effort would be directed at developing a true understanding of the subject without any extra white noise. There would be no bureaucratic hurdles and no unnecessary and tedious assignments, but just assignments that would ensure that the student become excellent in that particular area. The learning would be focused and efficient, with time to rest and play when the work was finished, and there would be no grades.

In the above cases, there simply wouldn't be a need or place for a letter grade. This was where education began, so one should ask how we ended up where we are today.

While this specialty type of learning might be inhibitive in that it offers only a very narrow range of expertise, it is at least closer to what can be considered a valuable education. Today it is hard to make a case that a lot of what we learn and are assessed on is of any real value at all. As was discussed in the chapter on curriculum, much of what has been deemed important curriculum simply is not.

So, even if you are unwilling to let go of the very specific goal of a certain G.P.A., it serves to understand the uncertain nature of grades in school today, and when the topic comes up with your child, it might make sense to not state expectations along these lines. It seems more productive to ask them what they are enjoying and what they find frustrating. It would be good to really look at a few graded assignments and to ask if the grading seems fair. It would be a shame to scold your child if the circumstances that surround a grading system are flawed. Again, by simply knowing that grading is not an objective science, but rather a subjective art, is half of the battle, and if we keep an eye on how our kids can grow up to be successful in a way that is realistic for them, no good or bad grade can inhibit our progress in that direction.

CHAPTER 12: CHEATING

THE MOST NATURAL TRANSITION OF topics is from grading to cheating, as one created the other. The following may sound like I am defending kids in the event that they are caught cheating, but I am. Well, maybe not defending them, but, again, using my extensive conversations with my tutoring students to explain the egregious act. I believe that you can spend time finding the reason behind cheating and can still condemn it.

First off, cheating is an expected act in school. The development of the first test back in the caveman days was probably followed by the first stand up divider to deter cheating, because the brightest caveman in the room probably invented cheating. Let's slow that down.

Ugbar, the teacher, decided that rather than doing cave drawings and showing them to the cave-kids, she would make them do the drawings themselves the following quarter moon (remember, time wasn't invented yet.) Teaching, in itself wasn't rewarding enough, so Ugbar decided that ranking kids in order of how good they were, or by how well they paid attention would add a whole new aspect to her job. Now she could be the teacher as well as the supreme judger of worth.

At any rate, the next quarter moon came up and each little cave student came to the board and had to recreate a dinosaur that had been stabbed in the neck with a widdled down piece of palm frond, (a lovely picture and a favorite of cave visitors.) One by one, the kids came up and failed miserably, except for a few. Finally Ugbar called on Barbutar, and rather than trying the impossible, Barbutar looked to his left and copied the good picture of the dinosaur with a stick in his neck exactly as he saw it. Barbutar unknowingly created the most commonly known way to succeed in a situation in which success is impossible today; cheating. On that same date, the cat and mouse game of kids cheating and teachers trying to catch them began. Fast forward this lovely scene of Ugbar and Barbutar a few bazillion years and here we are today. Now we have the same scene, but with nicer caves and harder tests. Sure the teachers have derived some fancy methods to stop Barbutar's prodigies, but everyone knows that kids are smarter than their adult counterparts.

Desk dividers and multiple forms of tests is no match for the creative intellect of kids. The following are some amazing ways that kids are able to cheat and get away with it. If you are a kid and are reading this book, congratulations on getting this far without dropping the book for a video game and please cover your eyes. I wouldn't want you to use this information for evil.

Okay, in order. You have the classic; look at your neighbors test. This one is the most commonly used and holds the most risk. For one, the kid next to you probably has little or no idea as to what they are doing, and secondly, you will for sure get caught. Most kids get caught in this way and this high prosecution rate gives teachers a false sense of accomplishment, allowing them to believe that they have nailed the Barbutars of the world.

The second most common method of cheating is the whole idea of bringing notes to class to refer to during the test. By the way, I've never met a professional in any arena that would work without references, so teachers, you've created this problem. If the kid was smart enough to create a cheat sheet that is pertinent to the chapter and will help them get an A, they deserve the A and you deserve to get tricked for not allowing the notes. Memorization has never and will never be considered important to either understanding or learning. The execution of the cheat sheet plan takes many forms and is proof of kids' creativity.

Obviously the note can be tucked into a sleeve, to be taken out when needed. The sleeve technique is a "go to" move for most kids, but lacks individuality. Some better hiding spots are on the inside of calculator covers, on the bottom of shoes and my favorite. One kid had the idea to partially peel off the label of a water bottle and write on the inside of it, only to re-stick it to the bottle again. Then, by peering through the bottle, he could read the answers from the far side of the bottle. That shouldn't be punished but should result in extra credit. That kid is a genius.

Another method, that for the record I have never employed, especially if my Algebra 1 teacher is reading this, is the imprinting method. You take a stack of twenty or so pieces of paper and use a ball point pen to write extremely firm on the top sheet. You can write key formulas or key notes as firmly as possible on the top sheet, and when you remove that top sheet the information is imprinted onto the following sheet, but is impossible to detect without careful inspection. Then, with a sweet smile and a twinkle in your eye, you pull out that supposed blank piece of paper to use for scratch work and you are home free. Just tilt the paper at the right angle and one can clearly read the imprinted notes.

Okay, if you are not impressed that kids are good at cheating, maybe we should have a discussion as to why it goes on. Most parents demand results, while not placing such a high priority on effort. Because the most common quote from parents of the kids that I tutor, again, is "we don't expect too much, just C's or B's." the goal has been laid out for the kid, without much in the way of constructive advice. While it is reasonable to shoot for such a grade, it is definitely a specific result that they are looking for. They didn't after all say " I just expect that my kid enjoy school and try." Not too many colleges look for the "just try" characteristic of kids and so we have set up a situation in which the bottom line is results.

If you are a kid that has been handed grades that are less than stellar for your whole life, you are less likely to "just try" only to be given the ceremonious slap in the face every semester at grades time. You might just outwit the system like the famed "Barbutar" and figure out a way to GET RESULTS. You know, often times cheating is most common with my best students. I know it sounds ridiculous, but it is true. The students that I tutor who have the highest grades cheat more often than my students with low grades, but they cheat in a way to not get caught.

As an example, by giving a classroom of thirty kids the same assignment of math problems, due the next day, ten percent of the kids do it and the other ninety percent copy it. Oddly enough, the kids that understand the game of school are the ones that cheat. Maybe they determine that an hour and a half of math problems, that they largely already understand, has to take second place to studying for a Spanish test. And as for the homework they skipped, they can "get it from" Suzie the next day during lunch. Given that each class assigns over an hour each night of homework, this might be the smartest way to approach one's workload. If you understand the math and don't have the time to jump through hoops for two hours, is the kid not allocating their time in the wisest manner? Should they skip dinner to do both assignments? Should they not be on the soccer team to do both?

One time I asked the kids to raise their hand if they had never cheated on a homework assignment in their lives, and because I have a good relationship with the kids and they felt as though they could be honest, not one hand went up. Everyone in the room had cheated before, including both my star students and my students that are less interested in school. Then, after an awkward silence, one of my funnier students raised his hand and tentatively said "Mr. Teves, everybody cheats."

As a tutor, I have the same insight and relationship with the kids to be able to get candid responses from them. After asking dozens of kids the same question, the figure that is starting to materialize is somewhere around a hundred percent of kids copy homework from time to time, while around fifty percent copy on a daily basis.

Frankly, the moment I worry the most about a kid is when they are so far gone that they don't even bother to copy homework anymore. It can actually be used as a measure of how much a kid cares about their academic success. The perfect little 4.0 student does, I repeat does, copy homework to maintain perfect grades, while the kid with bad grades doesn't cheat because he simply doesn't care.

Does the student who doesn't cheat get a little medal saying "you've done the right thing?" Is the non-cheater better off in this case? Does the A student get scolded for cutting corners? No. The A student gets applauded and accepted to a fine university and the other gets labeled as lazy. The A student GOT RESULTS and the other did not get results. We have trained these kids into thinking that school is about results.

Again, I don't say these things to support or defend cheating, but we reap what we sow, and we have sown, together, a climate where cheating is almost mandatory for the results that we so desire. If we had an honest interest in eliminating cheating from all schools, all of the time, we would remove the cause for it. Competitive grading and a lack of placing the priority on the effort of the kids will always ensure that cheating continues.

CHAPTER 13: ADD

ANOTHER HUGE TOPIC IN SCHOOLS, and that is almost entirely only existent in the school setting, is the condition of ADD and ADHD amongst our kids. The increasing prevalence of this apparent "disorder," I would argue, is a result of or byproduct of the demands being placed on kids in school, and of the unfair measurement of our kids that we have in place.

Understandably, the topic of ADD/ ADHD is a sensitive one, as many are dealing with this with their own children, and as a teacher in the classroom and a tutor in a one on one setting, I also have experience with the famed disorder. Because of the large volume of different cases that I have seen unfold over the years, with ADHD, I have some real insight into the issue. First of all, it is a good idea to attempt to define what ADHD is.

Taken from the AAFP, or American Family Physician website, (www.aafp.org/afp/20010501/1811ph.html) June, 2009, the following is the current working definition for ADHD. "ADHD, or attention-deficit/hyperactivity disorder, is a common health problem in children. Children with ADHD are hyperactive-they can't sit still. They are also impulsive and easily distracted. They have trouble coping at school and at home," the site explains.

With careful inspection, it is obvious that the above is less of a definition and more of a vague description, laced with subjectivity. Even by the clinical definition of ADHD, one could see how it might be difficult to accurately diagnose children with this disorder. Whereas most illnesses can be tested for using chemical tests, analyzing the presence or absence of certain proteins, bacteria, or hormones, this "health problem" is slippery and founded in opinion and speculation. Every statement pertaining to the symptoms of ADHD is subjective, and can be interpreted a thousand different ways by a thousand different people.

The site then goes on to display a chart, explaining "Things to look for if you think your child has ADHD." The chart is shown below.

Lack of Attention	Hyperactivity
Doesn't pay close attention to details	Often fidgets or squirms when sitting
Has trouble paying attention	Can't stay in seat
Doesn't seem to listen when spoken to	Runs about or climbs when he or she shouldn't
Fails to finish tasks	Can't play quietly
Has difficulty organizing tasks	Always "on the go"
Avoids tasks that need a lot of effort	Talks too much
Often loses things needed for home or school	Blurts out answers
Is easily distracted	Can't wait his or her turn
Is often forgetful	Often interrupts others

"Talks too much" is obviously not a concrete medical symptom. The above chart is a list of behaviors that are subject to different observations from different people. One teacher may find that the kid can't pay attention, while another more charismatic teacher might find that attention isn't a problem. Maybe the student talks too much in one class, but not in another because of how the seats are arranged or because they do or don't respect the authority of the teacher. Maybe one teacher has a higher threshold for student squirminess, whereas as the proverbial elderly librarian has a lower threshold for these types of behavior. Nothing in the above chart is an absolute that can realistically be measured.

The symptom from above that tells the story most clearly is the phrase "runs about or climbs when he or she shouldn't." How can we define times for when running and or climbing isn't appropriate? Would every person agree upon the same set of circumstances for which someone shouldn't run or climb? Maybe one person might think that in the morning, when we have fresh energy, it is the perfect time to run around and or climb. Maybe another person thinks that after lunch makes more sense, because we are exhausted from a long day of studying. Obviously they are suggesting that these things were happening in the classroom, which is uniformly considered inappropriate, but the reality is that most kids aren't in the classroom by choice.

Maybe the kid needs a greater percentage of time outside as opposed to a rigorous schedule of one class after another. I often wonder if I could survive the days that most kids go through in school today. Whatever your thoughts on the subject, or the thoughts of the next adult, it is absurd to suggest that this is any sort of scientific measurement.

And although naming behaviors in kids shouldn't in itself cause too much concern, it is the fact that diagnosis often leads to medication that is worrisome. Once a kid is given the title of having ADD or ADHD, the next most logical discussion is along the lines of how to best treat the patient. A vague and nondescript test, monitored largely by overworked and tired teachers, is no way to make intelligent decisions about issues as profound as medically treating growing children. As stated above, a healthy increase in the physical activity of the kids would seem a more logical step for improving focus than putting together cocktails of drugs until a mixture that provides a well behaved kid is found.

Then, above and beyond the risks of medicating these kids, is the issue of the stigma being given to the child. No matter how delicately a doctor puts it, a medical treatment is prescribed to solve a problem or treat a disease. Your child understands this and so do his or her peers. There is no such thing as a normal child, I've learned over the years, but attaching such a label to any child in such a hasty manner is cruel and not just.

While there are no doubt very methodical doctors that don't throw around the ADHD term easily, there are an infinite number of teachers that play doctor and will throw the ADHD card at your child without hesitation. It is a fact that many times the seed of the possibility that a child may have ADHD is planted by a teacher who is tired of the effort it takes to control kids. Naturally, some kids are less than excited at the prospect of sitting still through a large part of their childhood, so a conflict between the teacher and student will inevitably exist.

It is absurd to think that teachers have any sort of medical understanding or training that would give them the credentials to diagnose kids in this way, but all it takes is the issue being brought up, and the ball begins rolling. I have heard teachers say time and time again things like "God... that kid is so annoying. He just can't sit still," which in itself is not a crime. But to then go on to start an investigation into what disability the kid may or may not have certainly is a crime.

Then, just as is the case with taking your car to a mechanic, these psychologist and pediatric doctors are always willing to label a problem. I dare you to do just that; take your car to the local mechanic and ask, "is there anything wrong?" You will be sent home with a list of things to repair.

This is much the same as sending your kid to a psychologist or doctor for restless behavior. It then becomes the doctor's job to fix the problem. Your kid is restless in school and it is now on the doctor to fix that. Never mind if being restless is normal, or if the teacher is exceptionally boring, we are going to FIX your kid.

Kids are kids, but in the classroom they are expected to behave otherwise. To a certain degree, we should expect a level of squirminess and even a degree of lack of focus on a particular subject. Have you ever asked a puppy to sit still and not to chew on anything for ten seconds straight? Did the puppy do pretty well? Did the puppy realize that it is inappropriate to behave recklessly, apologize, and then do just as he or she was told? Did the puppy say, "you know, you are right... indoors is no place for acting wild and it is certainly no place to mark one's territory;" of course not. Now do the same experiment with an older golden retriever.

If you ask a puppy to act like a geriatric dog, it won't work. This point needs to be made as clearly as possible. Teachers in America are asking kids to act like middle aged businessmen and women from the fourth grade on. While this is certainly a ridiculous request, it becomes a heinous crime when we begin to drug our kids to get the results we are looking for.

Because almost every case of ADHD originates from a teacher complaining about behavior in class, the ADHD questionnaire is actually designed for teachers to fill out and includes questions about classroom behavior. Below is an actual questionnaire that a pediatrician sent to me to be filled out and returned.

Teacher

Date: _____

Circle day   M T W TH F
Of the week:

ADHD RATING SCALE

Information from this rating scale will help us learn about this child's behaviors across situations and across time. Please complete a form at the end of each day for five days, and note any issues that might have effected his/her behavior for that day, or other observations you think would be helpful. Thank You.

Child's Name   Age_____   Grade_____

Completed by   Date of observation _____

Circle the number in the one column that best describes the child.

	Not at all	Just a little	Pretty much	Very much
1. Often fidgets or squirms in his seat.	0	1	2	3
2. Has difficulty remaining seated.	0	1	2	3
3. Is easily distracted.	0	1	2	3
4. Has difficulty awaiting his turn in groups.	0	1	2	3
5. Often blurts our answers to questions.	0	1	2	3
6. Has difficulty following instructions.	0	1	2	3
7. Has difficulty sustaining attention to tasks.	0	1	2	3
8. Often shifts from one uncompleted task to another.	0	1	2	3
9. Has difficulty playing quietly.	0	1	2	3
10. Often talks excessively.	0	1	2	3
11. Often interrupts or intrudes on others.	0	1	2	3
12. Often does not seem to listen.	0	1	2	3
13. Often loses things necessary for class.	0	1	2	3
14. Often engages in physically dangerous activities without considering consequences.	0	1	2	3

Comments:

"Does your kid have a hard time sitting through an entire lecture?" Maybe the questionnaire should ask "does your kid's teacher lecture in a monotone voice and make an entire room full of kids want to shovel horse manure rather than be present?" Can we prescribe medicine to make these teachers more exciting? If the answer is no, then don't try to prescribe medicine for kids so that they stare fixedly at a boring teacher.

This being said, I would be a hypocrite if I didn't admit that there are kids that make teaching unbelievably difficult, but this is precisely the point. Numbing these active kids is only a plus for the teacher. Teachers shout ADHD because it is tiresome to chase a kid around all day trying to keep them on task. The question, though, is if you want your kid to be handed medicine to make his or her teacher's career easier? I don't know about you but I am only interested in the well being of my daughters and wouldn't think of tampering with their physiological processes so that some tenured teacher has an easier day; no way.

Often times the kids that are diagnosed with ADHD are totally hilarious and can be complete geniuses. I'm sure they aren't quiet in the library and might stray from the single file line they were supposed to be in, but what is our goal for our kids again? Was the goal to see them behave like a good little sheep or was it for them to fill their own shoes with wild individuality and creativity. My mind is made up. A report card full of D's is better than the prospect of literally handing my child medications to make their classroom a quieter place.

Then with some patience, at the pace that the natural growing process has deemed normal, that boy or girl will mellow out and no doubt become a productive adult. I can only be thankful that ADHD wasn't the cool thing when I was in school, as they would have stapled that tag to my sweatshirt without a second's thought. I can almost see my mom now, "really, do you really think he will get A's and not giggle in class if I give him these pills?" The thought is unnerving.

To take this discussion in another direction, how many adults do you think are diagnosed with ADHD per year? What percentage do you think that is of the total diagnosis of all individuals? Compared to kids, ADHD in adults is almost non-existent. The same trend is true about the prevalence of ADHD in girls versus boys. ADHD is diagnosed far more often in boys than in girls. So if young girls and adults of either gender basically can't acquire this famed ailment, maybe we should ask ourselves a simple question. What is our problem with boys? Let's just let boys be boys.

Here is another interesting fact about ADHD. To quote Denise Witmer, from Parenting of Adolescents Magazine, " A huge percentage of kids diagnosed with ADHD come from affluent homes." The article then went on to attempt to analyze the potential extra risks that kids from these homes would face, putting them at a higher level of diagnosis. Could it be the video games, the big screen TV's, etc.?

The article continues "Among children with a diagnosis of only ADHD, boys were nearly three times as likely as girls to have this diagnosis. White non-Hispanic children were more than twice as likely as Hispanic and black non-Hispanic children to report a diagnosis of ADHD. In addition, access to health care plays an important role in the diagnosis and treatment of ADHD. Children with health insurance coverage were more often reported to have a diagnosis of ADHD than children without health insurance coverage. "

The above article is an absurd statement of the obvious, and points out clearly how subjective the diagnosis process is. If a person seeks out the diagnosis, they will get it. Of course kids who are wealthy and have health insurance are more likely to be diagnosed with ADHD, as that little trip to the pediatrician might not have been a priority for another, less affluent, family.

This reminded me of an article my wife and I spent hours laughing about that showed how wealthy women were statistically prone to higher rates of depression. While someone's suffering should not be the subject of one's laughter, the logic behind that statement is what we found to be so funny. Certainly there can't be higher rates of depression in wealthy women, but merely a higher likelihood of that depression being diagnosed or even being discussed.

How often do women in third world countries make a quick visit to the doctor to say that they just aren't satisfied with all of the cars and houses? Women in third world nations are likely just a little bit tied up with trying to feed their families and fight off life threatening conditions. Maybe the issue of the size of their ankles or the newly arrived wrinkles can wait for a few minutes, while they try to figure out how to immunize their children from disease. To be clear, the diagnosis of depression is a luxury that the poor simply can't afford. The diagnosis of ADHD is the same.

In the case of the diagnosis of ADHD existing in higher rates amongst the wealthy, it is not these valuable contraptions like T.V. and videogames causing a particular problem, but rather it is the extra resources that these families have to serve pursuits like an explanation for why their ten year old son doesn't like sitting still.

One kid I tutor, who by the way is awesome, told me that he was sent home from the doctor with pills aimed at curing him from ADHD. As is normally the case, the process began with teachers complaining to his parents about his lack of focus or interest in their class. Again, never mind the effectiveness of the teachers or whether or not they were engaging, the goal was to have this child sit still.

This kid's dad, though, responded to the doctor's recommendation by throwing the pills in the nearest garbage can in a declaration that he would not numb his kid down with meds so that he would sit still in class. I salute this dad, because frankly, the answer to his son's ADHD questionnaire was probably all "Yeses."

If I sat this kid in front of you today, as a senior in high school, you would be appalled at the story I just told. He is funny, cool, smart, handsome, and successful.

Apparently, Mr. or Mrs. "whatever" was sick of telling this particular child not to draw on his desk, passed the news to Dr. "who ever", and the ball got rolling. Sixty five pills in the garbage of the family's house later, and the family made the right decision. Maybe a cure for the above situation is that Mr. or Mrs. "whatever" gets a job that guarantees the absence of kids and that her old job is given to a person who admires the energy only found in our kids.

And again, I should dilute my passion for the above subject a little and let it be known that there are certainly extreme cases that may make my rant seem irresponsible. In the event that a young person literally can't attend school or any public place for that matter without some assistance of a chemical, this can be understood. There are real issues that are treated with real medications, but I'd like to let the world know that the particular issue of ADHD is being tossed around wildly and without control. The cases of real need are far outweighed by those that aren't.

And to offer an alternative, rather than just defaming the efforts of others, I suggest some good old fashion exercise. Let's see how hyper little Billy is after he has run two miles. I had a kid on one of my science camps that had been labeled as the kind of kid that was hard to manage in class and I laughed out loud when I saw what happened upon his release into nature. We did a science trip to a beach with wide open sand dunes and this kid took off like a caribou. That is not an analogy, but he actually looked like a caribou. Not only did he run fast, he sustained this speed for miles.

By the way, would it surprise you to know that the year he joined the cross country team was the same year he had a major turn around in grades? Of course there were certainly other factors in his success, like age itself, but some kids flat out need to run as a priority that comes before even eating sometimes. If you are a teacher or a parent and are trying to stamp the wiggling out of a kid, please for us all, try to run them around the block ten times before you hand them a pill that you know nothing about. It is irresponsible to the kid and is just plain wrong.

And what are the medications being used today? Currently, the medicines most commonly used to treat ADHD fall under three classes. The three major groups are stimulants, non-stimulants, and others. From these three, however, it is my experience that the stimulants are prescribed the most often.

And before I list the drugs, as the list will likely bore you, I'd like to point out that the majority of Americans today are being treated for ADHD, as it is defined as a difficulty in focus and staying on task. Again, including you, likely, most Americans are being chemically treated to increase focus.

Just as kids with ADHD are often treated with chemical stimulants, you are likely under a strict daily stimulant treatment regimen as well. The stimulant I am referring to, of course, that stamps out the lack of focus in us all, is coffee. Let this point be in no way unclear. You are actively treating yourself with a stimulant every time you drink coffee, and depending on the age of the child, I recommend this type of treatment far before prescription medications.

As for the prescription medications being used today, the stimulants approved for use in kids over 6 years old include:

Adderall and adderall XR
Concerta
Cyclert
Dexedrine
Focalin
Metadata CD and Metadate ER
Methlin
Ritalin, Ritalin LA

The non-stimulant, passed in 2003, is Strattera. This is used in adults, children and adolescents. Then, if neither stimulants nor strattera work, other potential medications include:

Pamelor or other antidepressants
Catapres or Tenex
Wellbutrin
Effexor

* taken from MedicineNet.com on 1/28/09 (www.medicinenet.com/script/main/art.asp?articlekey=41895)

The site goes on to describe the side effects as being:

Decreased appetite/weight loss
Sleep problems
Headaches
Jitteriness
Social withdrawal
Stomachaches

Aside from the medical and symptomatic discussion of ADHD is the social one. As ADHD becomes more and more of a household name, a new social dynamic is starting to form. With the whole phenomena of the recent explosion of ADHD diagnosis, the stigma is dying down a little due to how common the alleged ailment is, and now kids are using it as an explanation for why they might not engage an academic activity. In just one day I might hear from three kids that they can't focus because "I have ADD." While some state this in a mocking tone, many try to make a legitimate case that they shouldn't have to sit down because they have clinical proof that they can't.

While I usually don't give their comment two seconds of thought before I yell at them to "get crackin," it is an interesting point. If a kid has asthma, they may be excused from running the mile. Along these lines, should a kid with ADHD be allowed to skip math class? Math class is very demanding with regards to focus and attention, and thus is not for the kid with ADHD. Leave it to teenagers to exploit any angle they can to get out of work.

But, even though ADHD is suspect with regards to the accuracy of its diagnosis, the fact is that we as teachers have to do what we can to make the classroom a more exciting and pleasant place to be. It is in the best interest of the kids and the teachers themselves to have everyone excited to be present. Along these lines, the climate created in the classroom can be a larger part of the solution for the prevalence of ADHD than even treatment itself.

Similarly, parents have the equivalent responsibility of creating a space or program at home that is suitable for the success of the student. I have a feeling that the images you just conjured up in your head for the right space for learning might be a little skewed from what I had in mind. If you were imagining a silent room with a desk and a pencil, we disagree on that point. If you had imagined no music and no distractions, again, we disagree. I'll describe to you the climate of my learning center, with all of its lizards, posters, and rock and roll, and explain why this is absolutely a more productive place to be for kids.

For the kid without ADHD, but that still finds homework to be tedious and painstaking, a few rules are important. First of all, the number one enemy to the productivity of kids is not distraction, but boredom. Whatever policies you do or don't have in place for how you have your kids do their homework, your primary concern should be whether or not your kid will likely become bored. A bored kid is not a productive kid.

When I started tutoring, I tutored a kid in a library, under the skeptical and watchful gaze of a librarian. We kept things hushed, there wasn't a peep around us, and the experience was a complete disaster. The kid looked like he wanted to kill himself, and what was even more worrying was that he gave me a few glances like he wanted to kill me. Complete silence, despite what was considered to make sense in 1953, is not conducive to studying.

After that I quickly switched to coffee shops to tutor, complete with music and the hustle and bustle that goes on in these places. People walk in and out, there are college kids and academics everywhere, and if things go well, someone might even spill a drink. What I found was that having several little tiny breaks, even between each math problem for instance, formed the recipe for higher productivity.

What we would typically do is cover one or two problems, look to our left to make a funny comment about a particular situation that might be brewing, only to return to our work to get a few more done. In this way, the time would fly and at no time would the kid feel the "B word," boredom. Again, boredom is the single most common culprit for academic failure.

And for the record, this understanding actually stemmed from my own success in college, and maybe if you look back, yours as well. I found, and I might have been classified as an ADHD kid in the hands of the wrong doctor, that I would work sluggishly at home. I would get a few things done, quickly become bored, and certainly not be able to sustain a high level of focus for long. On the contrary, though, if I would sit down in a hopping coffee shop, with my self prescribed stimulant (coffee,) I could study for hours and have a great time while doing it. And, if you have any doubts as to this theory of coffee shop productivity, just go to your neighborhood coffee shop any night of the week. What you will see is several laptops with several young academics behind them. And most key of all, none of those kids will have a look on their face that would lead you to think that they need professional help. Rather, they all will look pretty content and involved in their studies.

So, if you have a kid that is teetering on the edge of being labeled as having ADHD, or even if you have a kid that has already been given that title, DO NOT set them in your kitchen with a pencil and tell them to get busy. Give them their i-pod, give them some excitement, or drop them off at Borders while you look at books. Remember, your policy of protecting them from distractions hasn't paid off, right, so try this. I don't even attempt to grade papers without a movie in front of me, because I know I'll throw in the towel six papers in. By having something going on to keep me interested, even as just noise in the background, I can grade papers for hours. Your kids are likely the same.

What is not a good plan of action is to succumb to the enormous pressure that a teacher or pediatrician can put on a parent to medically treat their child. Given the subjective nature of how ADHD is diagnosed, and then consequently treated, it is prudent for a parent to hear the complaints and recommendations of teachers or doctors with a healthy amount of skepticism. Remember that most cases of ADHD begin with the frustrations of tired teachers, which in itself is largely opinion and emotion based.

There are many alternatives to medical treatment for the age old dilemma of kids being restless in school, including choosing a class or school that simply allows for more movement. What should not be the first choice of action for a child like this is a trip to the local doctor to pick a drug. ADHD, whether real or perceived, is certainly not an indicator to future success, so as a parent, its mention should not be greeted with the same disappointment as a medical disorder. If one remembers that the person to benefit the most from a medically treated child is a tenured teacher, it becomes easier put the situation in perspective.

CHAPTER 14: SAT

GAIN, ANOTHER INCREMENT OF PRESSURE added to the workload of the kids is the famed SAT. Along the lines of getting results, success in one's classes is not, in itself, enough, as a student must also be successful on a standardized test designed to remove the subjectivity in school. That test, required by all students interested in attending a four year university, is the SAT.

Perhaps the most feared and respected acronym in the academic world of high school students, the SAT is one of the most discussed tests at the block party, when parents are beginning to wonder as to the future success of their kids. This test, originally an acronym for "Scholastic Aptitude Test," makes a lot of sense, as it is an objective measure of kids in a very subjective field. Where there is essentially no continuity from school to school with regards to grading and difficulty in curriculum, the derivation of the SAT was an attempt to bring sanity into the system.

The SAT is basically a test designed to take a "snapshot" of a kid with regards to his or her understanding in the areas of math, reading comprehension, and writing. This, at face value, can only be seen as a positive thing, even though it may cause anxiety and resentment for those who score less than stellar.

The test, as it stands now with some recent changes, has three sections. The total test is 3 hours and 45 min. and the sections are reading, writing, and math. The table below shows the literal breakdown of the sections, including length and number of questions.

The Section	Question Type	Time
Reading- 3 Parts	19 Sentence Completions	
	48 Reading Comprehension	

	67 Total Questions	70 min.
Writing- 3 Parts	49 Grammar	
	1 Essay	
	49 Total Questions + Essay	60 min.
Math- 3 Parts	44 Multiple-choice	
	10 Grid-ins	
	54 Total Questions	70 min.

With regards to how the test is scored, each section; math, reading, and writing, have a total points range of 200 to 800. What they say is that the average score for each section is 500, so an average total score would be 1500. Then, in order to figure out the percentile ranking that is given, in addition to your score, the value given is the percent of the kids that scored beneath you. That is, if you have scored in the 60th percentile, that means 60 out of 100 of every kids scored below you.

The SAT is given seven times per year, usually between October and June, on Saturday mornings, and it is certainly okay to take the test several times. The only thing, allegedly, is that if a kid takes the test several times until their score is high enough for their liking, some colleges will average the scores, rather than simply taking the highest score. Other universities and colleges might only consider the highest score, so for a definite answer, one would have to talk directly with the school of interest.

When considering the daunting task of preparing for the SAT, there are some things that one should take into consideration. First off, there are absolutely programs and courses that will increase the number score for your child. Without getting into the names of private companies that offer these SAT "boot camps," the majority of the programs happens over a few weekends and do make real gains.

By simply sitting your child down and forcing him or her to take several practice exams repeatedly, tangible progress can already begin to happen. Then, with some tips and, again, some tedious repetition, your kid can also become relatively adept at throwing together an essay in the short period of time allowed on the SAT. In this way, these programs are pretty successful and I can attest to the fact that students of mine who have taken the courses have in fact seen increases in their SAT scores.

If money is an issue, though, it is my opinion that any parent can simulate a similar program at home, as long as the kid is on board and actively participates. There are certainly books that offer practice tests, and if your child does all of them, regardless of how well they do on the practice tests, they will benefit instantly.

As far as a strategic approach to taking the SAT, there are some methods that make sense and some that don't. To address the rumor that it does not pay to guess on the SAT, this is actually the truth. There is a penalty, although not huge, for guessing incorrectly on a question. Therefore, if a kid has no idea as to a particular problem, they should skip it rather than gamble. Supposedly, although this is slightly subjective, the questions are said to be arranged with growing difficulty, so that one should understand the earlier ones and might want to skip the last ones. The reality is that you should do the ones you know and leave the ones you don't know alone.

There are more tips for outwitting the test, offered by many of these SAT "boot camps," but these cute little techniques can not correct a lifetime of academic neglect. Essentially, some tactics suggest that if two of the five potential answers are similar, and the other three are completely different, it is likely one of those two similar ones. Now your odds are 50% of getting it right. Does that sound like a conservative practice? I don't think so either.

To make a huge difference, however, in how one does on the SAT, it is important to understand what the test aims to do. Rather than a measure of understanding of academic subjects, I consider the SAT to be a measure of lifestyle. What I mean is that the SAT is able to distinguish between someone who has been cranial for their entire life and has considered academics to be a priority, from someone who has had other priorities. More simply put, if a child has never been an academic at heart, there is no prep class in the world that will allow him or her to give an impression other than that on the test.

As an example, for the vocabulary section of the test, there is no way that a kid can coincidentally study the exact words that will be on the test. A class might be able to provide clues by teaching Latin prefixes, or by showing some basic patterns, but there is no replacement for having a kid who has simply been a life time reader. The kid that has been reading book to book since the day they were able to read will always outscore the kid who took an SAT course, yet has never read a book for pleasure. This is what is meant by my statement that the SAT is a measure of lifestyle rather than academic retention.

Similarly, for the rare kid who enjoyed math and was not content with not knowing certain concepts, he or she will undoubtedly do better on the test than someone who spent their youth resenting math. The student who excelled in sports maybe, or other activities like music or theater, but that couldn't wait to put the math book away will not be able to pretend to be super knowledgeable in math because of a weekend course. A course like this can incrementally increase the number value of a kids score on the SAT, but can not imply a lifestyle that the kid did not live.

So, for a very sincere and complete answer to the question of what a student should do to prepare for the SAT, you should insist that your kid always read, regardless of the content of the book, starting at a very early age. I plan to allow my girls to read the books of their choice, barring the obvious extreme materials, but will demand that they do indeed read. There is no replacement for the lifelong learning and the handle on the English language that comes along with being a "reader."

Similarly, if you would like to prepare your kid for the math part of the SAT, it has to start in the first grade. You would have to be supportive the whole way through, with regards to math, and can never have been quoted as saying "I hated math as a kid," or "sorry, I suck at math. You are on your own." These attitudes are contagious and deliver the message that math isn't important. And maybe the message that math isn't important was exactly what was meant by the comments, but this definitely won't help SAT scores.

This being said, SAT scores certainly are not everything. If you haven't had these academic ideals as the number one or even number two priorities in your household, so what. There are many things that I deem more important for my girls than a proficiency in math. There is no shame in raising a family that is strong, healthy, and happy, but that score less than the offspring of the Jones' from next door. And what is funny about my statements about encouraging reading with my children, is that an SAT score is not even the smallest of factors in my interest in their reading.

I asked one concerned father, when pressed about how low his son might score on the SAT, if he would trade a few things for a better score. I told him about one kid from one of my classes that was the result of a very cranial family, and who was shockingly astute in school and would likely ace the SAT. This child, though, was very obese. That is, while his family had a focus on learning, which is certainly a positive thing, they had no focus on exercise or even a healthy diet. I asked this concerned father if he would trade the childhood of health and activity that he gave his son, for the childhood from the above example. He answered with a resounding no.

While there is obviously no correlation between strength in academics and an unhealthy lifestyle, obviously, the example serves as an oversimplified case to make a good point. We all raise our kids with what we consider to be important priorities and ideals. Often times, our kids do exactly as we do, regardless of our verbal instructions and rather than fight this concept, parents should embrace it. In the case of the SAT, the same logic holds. Your kid has brilliant strengths and those strengths will lead to his or her eventual success, so it is absurd to lose sleep over a silly test. The minute you do begin to stress, ask yourself what changes in your child that you would be willing to accept for a few more points on the SAT.

It is also counterproductive to pass this stress on to your child and to demand higher scores, understanding that knowledge for that particular test is accumulated over years, rather than days. Remember, they were raised in the fashion of the life that you live, and are scoring accordingly. Be proud of their positive attributes and don't worry about what they don't have.

CHAPTER 15: SCHOOLS ARE INEFFICIENT AND BUREAUCRATIC

A S THE GOAL, AGAIN, IS to find the culprit for the ineffectiveness of our schools, a huge portion of the blame needs to be directed towards how schools are run, in an administrative sense. While the philosophical faults of our curriculum are the fundamental reason that many kids are not content with our schools, the bureaucratic way in which they are run would make it nearly impossible for any model to be successful. In a purely business sense, from the top offices to the classrooms, schools are intensely inefficient. This inefficiency is not just noteworthy, but shocking. Behind every door and in every corner of our public schools is a pocket of wasted resources.

The reason for this tremendous amount of waste might be the nature of public schools themselves. Public schools are essentially a centrally planned organization. Public schools don't make decisions based upon market trends, but rather the decisions are made by central planners that do their best to diagnosis the needs of schools and then meet them. The failure of the "from the top down" nature of how we run schools and the school districts, demonstrates the inherent flaws in having a centrally controlled organization and is why we as Americans largely accept that having the market drive most aspects of our society is more effective.

Having a central body micromanage the operations of organizations has historically been proven to be the least efficient way to run things. Because there is constant pressure in an open market to improve and to earn the respect of your audience, things that are consumed based on their merits are always fresher and more creative than those created by central planners. This basic tenet of how we do things in America should not only apply just to tennis shoes, ipods, movies, and cars, but should also apply to our educational institutions as well. There should be a large pressure for them to remain relevant and fresh.

And if one believes that there is a fundamental difference between education and products for sale, a good question would be as to how the Nature Channel is successful. There are educational shows that teach kids facets of science and leave kids fighting for space in front of the t.v. to learn. There is certainly no requirement that kids watch the Nature Channel or shows like CSI, but rather the channels have to earn their audience. For this reason, they are consistently performing and offer an outstanding product. Public schools, on the other hand, do not have to earn the attention of their audience, and have therefore become lazy. Teachers and administrators don't act to impress their audience, but rather their bosses.

On the contrary, for private schools there is no mandate that certain kids attend their schools. That is, zoning has no effect on the attendance of private schools, so each and every family that attends the school has to make the decision on their own to actually pay dues and go there. This decision is obviously based on the merits of the school and on the actual successes the school has produced previously. If the school stops performing, attendance will drop and the school will be closed.

Such a pressure does not exist on public schools, and thus, they are often much lower achieving. The federal government has tried to set out its own pressures to have the schools perform, but these, having been centrally planned, have missed the mark. The market is the best judger of worth and always has been.

Another characteristic of privately run organizations is that by the nature of competition, they are less likely to engage in expensive activities that do not yield results. A private organization has to tend to every expense and is likely to ask if the expense is necessary to achieve the goals of the organization. If it is not, the business will do without that particular expense. Because of this, privately run organizations are automatically more efficient than public ones, and will fail if they are not.

Private schools are also not subject to red tape that lacks common sense. The best example of this red tape is how a teaching certificate is required to teach for any public school, regardless of education or experience. While this sounds like an intelligent practice and doesn't ring any alarm bells upon first hearing it, the policy has backfired and given private schools an advantage over public schools.

At a private school in which I worked in Hawaii, we had two teachers with PhDs. These were brilliant teachers that the students loved, and that had a complete mastery of their subjects. These teachers, though, couldn't be hired at a public school because they lacked certificates. A person with a PhD can teach at the finest universities in the world, but because of red tape passed by legislators, they simply can not be hired to teach at a public high school.

So, if a principal of a public school finds that the PhD is the best applicant by far, they, again, are powerless to make the right decision. The result is that a lesser candidate is accepted to teach our kids for the mere fact that central planning has resulted in a rule to which an exception is not an option. Obviously a private school could make an on the spot decision to take the best applicant, and they do, to the advantage of their students.

Because not all families can afford private schools, though, the discussion will be kept on public schools and their behaviors. The efficiency of private schools is still a worthy discussion, however, as it sets the stage eloquently for a discussion on the inefficiency of public schools.

Chapter 16: The CLAD

I N REVIEWING MY OWN EXPERIENCES over the last few years with regards to teaching, several situations have arisen that exemplify the waste that is so common in our schools. In particular, the CLAD certification, the new teacher project, and mandatory professional development stand out as the most obvious.

The CLAD (Cross-cultural Language and Academic Development) certification process, required for all teachers in California, is a frustrating example of a squandering of resources in public schools. At some point, due to low scores amongst ELD (English Language Development) students, the state decided to find a solution that would bring the scores of these students up.

While the goal here is noble and one couldn't find fault in such a desire, the response was irrational. Like only a centrally planned organization can do, the state mandated that all teachers enter into a training program that would supposedly educate teachers on how to address the needs of these kids. Regardless of the socioeconomic, family, or home-life situation of the kids, the scores of these students would then magically rise with the presence of certificates on all of the walls of California teachers. As you can imagine, the proposed solution was simple while the problem is complex, so the trainings were ineffective. By a certain date, however, all new teachers could only be hired upon their completion of the training, and existing teachers had to comply to be eligible for rehire.

The CLAD program is essentially just internet coursework designed to teach the latest theories and research in the instruction of English language development. To be put more clearly, there is the idea that immigrants, for whom English is not their first language, would benefit from a certain style of teaching, and this program has filled the heroic role of teaching teachers how to do this. To date, there are two ways to become CLAD-certified.

One can either try to pass a test on the material to become CLAD certified or take online course work, but the hoops must be jumped through if one would like to stay in the teaching profession. If, however, a teacher can't take the test in time, they can pay fifty five dollars and receive an emergency CLAD and retain their job. The emergency CLAD is paper work and in no way benefits Spanish speaking students, but was somehow determined to have value.

Then, because of the power of the teacher's unions and the desire of departments of education in the state to remain competitive, the school districts themselves have ended up absorbing the cost of sending all of their veteran teachers, and new hires, through the CLAD program. So in an already resource deficient field, like public education, administrators were given a new set of mandatory expenses. And to be clear, these costs are exorbitant. To just take the written test, registration is more than five hundred dollars, and completing the coursework through classes is even higher. Multiply this number by every teacher, in every district in California, and you'll have an estimate as to the size of the waste currently happening.

And if the CLAD certification was a success in closing the socioeconomic gap amongst all students, no cost would be too high. On the contrary, the program is literally an exercise in jumping though hoops, both for administrators and the teachers taking the curriculum. Having just taken the CLAD test and passed, I can clearly state that the process did not enhance my understanding of how to reach immigrant students. Examples of the lessons from this curriculum were ideas like "if you have parties with food from the countries of the ELD kids, they will feel at home and are more likely to learn." Whether or not this is true, it is certainly not something that California can afford to be spending millions and millions of dollars on.

Having done this, though, the administrators of districts can not be accused of doing nothing, and have temporarily escaped criticism with regards to the performance of ELD kids. It seems that all too often, focus groups and quickly thrown together legislation is designed, not to address the real needs of kids, but to show the greater audience that a good old fashioned effort is being put in. This particular program, designed to show an attempt at helping ELD kids, again, is called the CLAD.

The irony is that if a teacher was born and raised in Mexico, and might be deemed by you or me to have the skills to deal with an English learner from Mexico, they are still not exempt from the CLAD certification. Then, if the Mexican born teacher lacks the CLAD certification, he or she will be let go to be replaced, potentially, by a white male from Kentucky who has passed the CLAD coursework and is therefore allegedly more suitable for the task of teaching kids from Mexico that don't speak English. So obviously, while the original intentions of helping ELD students may have been sincere, the program has become self-serving and has strayed from its original intent.

On a personal note, I have often been the only Spanish speaker in a department since I began teaching, but was the last to receive CLAD certification and faced potential removal if I didn't act fast. My administrators intentionally gave me the students that didn't speak English, but informed me that if I didn't get the CLAD, I wouldn't be invited back. Ironically, the rooms around me were full of CLAD certified teachers that did not speak a single word of Spanish. Who do you think would be more likely to serve this population of Spanish speakers? Whatever one's feelings, this expense simply doesn't make sense for schools. Certainly these higher costs are a detriment to all students, regardless of their primary language. Do you think that private schools require CLAD certification for all of their teachers?

Chapter 17: The New Teacher Project

UCH THE SAME AS THE CLAD certification and another example of absurd waste in the public schools, there is a mandatory "new teacher project," in the state of California. A new teacher or a teacher certified in another state that wants to move their credential to California is forced to enroll in a costly two year program to "clear their credential." This program is in addition to the teaching certificate and the student teaching hours that the applicant has already had to do to satisfy their degree to become a teacher in the first place. Like so many other programs in teaching, the above has become a self-serving piece of red tape with little to no value, but that costs thousands of dollars for each teacher to complete. And like the CLAD, to remain competitive, the districts pay for the program rather than the teacher.

In my specific case, I asked if the three years of teaching in the classroom and the five years of running a learning center might exempt me from the program. The answer was "well it should, but sorry, it is a state wide policy." Again, only a centrally planned organization could give this type of answer. If a teacher has been teaching for twenty five years in a state other than California, they are still forced to go through a two year "new teacher" program to be able to teach in California, paid for by the district. No matter how absurd and wasteful this sounds, there is, again, no room for exceptions and so it continues to happen in the public school system today.

I pointed out to the woman in charge that this seemed to not make sense, but that because I recognized the value in screening teachers to make sure that they are of high caliber, I suggested that they sit in on my class to critique my abilities. I asked if there were not some objective way to determine whether or not I was able to serve the kids, and I was greeted with a frown and the same statement. The particular clerk was frustrated that I didn't get the simple point that it was a "policy," and that practical negotiations were not part of how things were done. Having come from the business world, this was particularly frustrating for me.

Then, because the program is mandatory, I began to meet with my "mentor." She proceeded to give me forms to fill out that would explain my goals for the coming year. When I asked what she meant by goals, she simply told me to pick a category and consider it my goal for the year, regardless of my sincere interests. She gave me the knowing look like "just pick one." The list included themes like addressing ELD students, and how to inspire high achievers. I then was told to write statements of intent down, explaining how I would address these goals and would likely have had to collect data to show that I was making an effort.

Right off the bat there seemed to be an unstated reality, known by us both, that the exercise was largely just red tape. Statements like "we just have to get this done," and "what they want to see is…" My mentor would periodically sit in on my classes and tell me "good job," or "I enjoyed the lecture on the stock market." While she was congenial and polite, this type of cost to the state can only be seen as wasteful.

Because we both understood that the red tape had to be dealt with, she would say things like "we have to meet for 4 hours per month and document, on paper, that we met." Typically we would spend the time with her asking me questions about my tutoring business or discussing random facets of our personal lives. And while I didn't resent her company, the program in its entirety was a huge waste of resources and time. Collaboration is essential for teaching, but it happens amongst colleagues and members of departments without cost. To mandate collaboration and assume a new financial burden to the state doesn't make sense.

The irony is that if a teacher elected not to do the new teacher project, it would be okay, but that they would have to finish the program within five years or be terminated. That is, a person can teach for three years without doing the program, but that in the last two years of that five year span, they would have to do it.

Again, if the program is so important, how can they trust a person to educate the kids for those three years without the training? Even the bureaucrats seem to understand that it is red tape and we need time to get the red tape dealt with. If this is so, why not just eliminate it altogether?

The reality is that a new teacher project might serve some people entering the career but that this type of help has to be sought out rather than forced. My description of the program was not to say that there is no value in any type of training program, but that where a policy is inflexible, it quickly becomes ridiculous. It is not the fact that teachers are given extra support in California that is of concern, but that the price tag for that support is exorbitant, with little value. Schools simply can't complain about a lack of funding while programs like these are still in place.

Chapter 18: Mandatory Professional Development

ANOTHER HUGE ARENA IN WHICH resources are wasted belligerently, and one that is cousin to the first two, is the field of mandatory professional development for teachers. Again, this seems to be an attempt at making noise to show that effort is being put forth for a certain issue rather than a genuine movement for change.

I have always been frustrated with problems that seem apparent to the masses, but that don't filter to the top administrative officials. That is, if you were to ask a teacher in your neighborhood about mandatory professional development, they would roll their eyes and release a sigh. And this resentment is not akin to a kid and vegetables, but rather stems from the absurd waste of time and energy that mandatory professional development has become.

Professional development is essentially a series of mandatory meetings, often led by an ex-teacher, that vary by department. That is, the PE department might attend a certain series of professional development meetings about one topic, while the math department attends another. The amount of professional development varies depending on the school district, but it is seldom voluntary.

The topics are typically designed to address some area of concern in schools, but as they are centrally planned, they often seem irrelevant to the teachers in attendance. Some examples of topics that I have seen personally are a discussion of which vocabulary words might be difficult for "English Learners," writing math vocabulary on the whiteboard before each day, and how to incorporate karate into a PE unit. And while these topics may be appealing to some people, schools pay exorbitant costs to make these meetings mandatory to their entire staff. This cost is not justifiable, particularly when the teachers forced to be at the meeting are resistant to the mandate.

Professional development seems okay philosophically, that teachers would improve upon their craft over time, but the plan has failed. How is it possible that teachers in every district and at every school resent professional development, yet policy makers continue to place value upon it?

Most teachers attend these so called professional development meetings with papers to grade, post cards to fill out, or some type of crossword puzzle to complete. Because professional development meetings are typically separated out by subject, stories of how ridiculous they may be vary from department to department. The best professional development meeting, reportedly, was for the physical education department in which they participated in kung fu classes. While this is pretty entertaining and no doubt was more exciting than the meetings for the history department, this can't be considered an essential cost. Schools often complain about a lack of funding, but I'd make the case that they do not, in any shape, use funds that they do have with any common sense.

For our math department, we were placed in front of a speaker, a couple of times per month, who began his discussion by apologizing for taking up so much of our time. Does anyone with any sense of pride in what they do apologize for using up your time? Do the hottest selling new release movies begin by apologizing for wasting your time? Once the ritualistic apology had been completed, he would then go on to promise with puppy dog eyes that he would finish on time, not a second over.

The content of his professional development meetings was something along the lines of reaching kids who lack academic vocabulary. He would do such engaging activities as to list words and ask us which words might be hard to understand for our students. We literally took turns saying words like "differentiate" and "speculate," and he would write them on the board.

There was absolutely no value in this process and I found myself constantly pondering how we could more wisely use the money that we were paying this "professional development" speaker. Eventually I asked if he was suggesting that we don't use these words, as the only way to learn words is by being introduced to them in context. He answered no. If we aren't going to avoid the words, and if nothing is going to be done about whether or not we utilize high level vocabulary words, can someone clear up for me why we are even listing them in the first place. The meetings were literally an exercise in complete insanity. Upon leaving such a meeting, it is hard to stomach statements from the district like "we are under-funded." Schools may be under-funded, but are unbelievably irresponsible with the resources that they do have.

The one valuable part of professional development is that I do enjoy to go to these meetings and observe how similar we as adults are to the kids we teach. I find that teachers will pretend to have to use the restroom, only to go outside to get a break, will sneak a text message in during meetings, and will even hide a book inside their supposed reading material to avoid the project at hand. I have seen teachers pass notes and even make jokes about the guest speaker's outfit or hairstyle. When teachers are forced to be in these meetings, they revert back to the fifteen year old versions of themselves.

Maybe the greatest value in the professional development meetings is that they are a lesson in what not to do in the classroom. Certainly if we ask our students to remain astute for an entire period or during a lecture, we should feel obligated to make sure that they aren't in as much discomfort as we are in during these meetings. If we interrupt with side conversations and don't pay attention so that we can correct papers, how can we ask our students to behave in a better manner than we are capable of?

Because this was probably not the intent of the creators of the professional development program, to show what not to do, I suggest they either be voluntary or scrapped entirely. As it stands now, the cost of renting the room and the cost of hiring the ex-teacher to offer active teachers irrelevant information is money that could be placed elsewhere with much more consequence.

CHAPTER 19: STAR TESTING

THE NEXT CULPRIT FOR INTENSE waste in public education is that of the STAR testing that happens every year in California. In the nature of bureaucracies and their inherent ability to create more white noise than tangible progress, the STAR testing program has been failed at best. But like most failed projects in public schools, the intentions, again, were relatively noble.

The desire to create and be able to measure equality amongst schools, regardless of geographic or cultural and socioeconomic boundaries is not evil, but actually makes sense and should be a priority. In a country as organized and successful as the United States of America, it wouldn't be acceptable to have pockets of mediocrity with regards to the public school system, along with pockets of excellence. It is in our nature to strive for equality.

It should also be in our nature, however, to act in a methodical and rational manner when it comes to the creation of policy. The STAR test, put on by the state of California each year, simply isn't based on reason. As a molecular biology major in college, I was taught that in order to pursue an answer to a scientific question, one had to remove all variables except for the one being measured. The STAR test does not do this.

With the STAR test, the question that the creators of the test set out to answer was how much is being learned by the students of the different schools within the state. The test was considered to be an objective comparative measure to judge how successful schools were in educating their kids. If we, as administrators and citizens aim to sincerely measure this, though, the test can only have that one variable. As it stands today, there are several variables in STAR testing.

The STAR testing (Standardized Testing and Reporting) is required of all students of California schools in elementary, middle, and high school and includes all basic subjects. The tests are based on California state academic standards and are completed using scantron forms, so as to facilitate easy grading. The test does not affect a student's GPA or any other facet of their academic record in any way, and is only used to measure the school that they attend.

Once word got out to the students, themselves, that there were no actual repercussions for poor performance on the test, the inherent flaw in the STAR test was exposed. "If I am not graded on this," the students reasoned, "why should I try?" This is where the subjectivity of the test comes in. The test is not a measure of student ability, but rather how effective schools are in getting their students to participate and to actually try on the statewide test.

At around the same time as the first administration of the STAR test, the cute little practice of filling in bubbles on the scantron form to make designs and pictures was invented. Students from the highest achieving schools to the lowest achieving schools alike have taken this concept to a new level. Many kids will brag openly that they put all C's, or that they bubbled in the image of a flower or a dolphin, knowing that their teacher or school administrators have no recourse. In fact, the administrators shouldn't even be aware of these designs, as they are prohibited from reviewing the answers of the students.

Because the consequences of poor results for a school on STAR testing are so severe for the school, though, a very real problem has arisen. Rather than an emphasis on the learning of the material on the star test itself, principals and schools have been reduced to essentially begging and bribing students into putting effort forth on the annual exam. Resources are being dumped into "enlightening" kids as to why they should try on the test, ice cream parties are promised, and individual teachers have begun to give incentives for participation.

Some teachers and schools have intelligent campaigns to get kids to try and other teachers and schools do not. Whatever the case, STAR testing was not invented for this purpose and the true meaning of the test has been lost. The test does not measure understanding in students, but rather all of these other factors. Again, this can in no way be considered a scientific approach to finding out a particular answer.

As tangible proof of how STAR testing can be grossly inaccurate, the case of a nearby high school, in a largely wealthy neighborhood, is a good example. For a test that matters to the kids, the high school exit exam, the kids from this wealthy neighborhood score off the charts. This particular high school has the highest local exit exam pass rate, mostly due to the affluent nature of the families and kids that attend the school. These kids understand that they can not graduate if they don't pass the exit exam and, therefore, have a built in incentive to be successful.

In contrast, however, this school embarrassingly has one of the lowest performance levels on the STAR test in the entire county. That is, other schools with relatively low exit exam pass rates are outperforming this affluent school on the STAR test. Because the content of the two exams is of the same nature, one can only attribute the low scores on one exam versus the high scores on the other as a lack of effort on the test that, in the minds of the students, "doesn't count." The kids from this affluent high school were obviously not putting effort forth, and in their minds, why should they? Many of the kids find the fact they that "put all C's" on the test to be funny. What is not funny, though, is that the school has been put on "probation" and may lose valuable funding as a result.

Whatever one's feelings may be about the kids who aren't trying on the exam, a more strict conviction should be put on the policy makers that find sense in this form of school wide assessment. It seems insane to me that an intelligent person in administration could not readily see the flaws in such logic and that the person could base very serious decisions, such as the allocation of funds to different schools, on the outcome of these tests. Can they really believe that the knowledge accumulation of the students is the only thing that determines their number score on the exam? Can they really believe that STAR testing is an objective measurement of a school's performance? STAR testing might be an accurate measure of the loyalty of the student body to their school, but it certainly doesn't serve to offer the information it was set out to collect.

A better question, though, is whether or not this is a wise use of resources. Because, again, schools are constantly crying out that they are underfunded, one has to question the rationale behind this type of careless spending. The amount of money that goes into the creation of the testing materials, the proctoring of the exams, the analysis of the results, and the energy put into pleading with kids to try, is absurdly wasteful. Even if all of these costs came to ten cents collectively, it would be a waste of ten cents, but the cost is exorbitant. This STAR test is not a wise use of money.

CHAPTER 20: THE DISTRIBUTION OF FUNDING

ASIDE FROM BUREAUCRATIC ACTIVITIES, WHAT might be the largest and most taxing use of funds is in how the funds are distributed, with a heavy imbalance directed towards special needs kids. The nature of the waste seems to be based on the simple assumption that everyone has to reach the exact same level in math, science, or any subject. More specifically, regardless of ability or interest, every kid has the same academic requirements. Trying to make this concept, which is contrary to how the world works, happen, is a frustrating process and is responsible for consuming a huge portion of the schools financial resources.

As reported in the Testimony before the Senate Appropriations Subcommittee for the District of Colombia, in 2002, by Andrew J. Rotherham, "spending is in the $35-$60 billion range annually. This means that the cost of educating students with special needs is 21.4 percent of K-12 spending in the U.S." While the cost is around 21%, the number of special needs kids is nowhere near that percentage. This is the imbalance. The numbers are slightly different today, but the trend remains the same, with an over-emphasis on funding being directed towards special needs students.

Similarly, in the report, "Per Student Cost Figures for The District of Columbia Public School System" by Mary Levy and, Washington Lawyers' Committee for Civil Rights & Urban Affairs, November 2007, a comparison is made between the cost of a general education student, an ESL student, and a specials needs student. The numbers are pretty interesting and show clearly how we as a society are directing our resources.

In 2008
General Education: $9,036 per pupil
ESL: $12,365 per pupil
Special Education: $19,953

These figures do NOT include other costs associated with special education, like the costs of transportation. When factoring in these additional costs, the price per student becomes ridiculous.

And what might be more troubling than the fact that we spend so much on special needs education, is just who is determined to be considered "special needs." Rather than an emphasis on physical disorders, much more unclear categories of disorders are becoming prevalent. The Testimony before the Senate Appropriations Subcommittee for the District of Columbia, by Andrew J. Rotherman went on to say "The 'learning disabilities' category has ballooned from 21.6 percent of students identified for special education in 1977 to 46.2 percent in 1998 and is now over 50 percent." That is, where the majority of disabilities in the past were easy to identify and were very clear, the bulk of our alleged special needs kids now are ailed by very vague disorders. I have had countless students that my fellow teachers and I consider to be completely capable, but based on attitude and behavior, rather than a learning disability, continue to fail. Because of the pattern of low performance, though, they are given a diagnosis and extra funding, often with little positive result.

As a specific example of this growing trend, the following is a breakdown of all of the special needs kids in a district in which I worked. Notice that some impairment is physical, with little room for subjectivity, while the largest numbers are found in categories that certainly are subjective, and could be diagnosed ten different ways by ten different people.

In 2010, in a district in California:
Mental retardation: 41 students
Hard of Hearing/ Deaf: 13 students
Speech/Language impairment: 30 students
Vision Impairment: 4 students
Emotional Disturbance: 81 students
Orthopedic Impairment: 16 students
Other Health Impairment (ADHD mostly): 102 students
Specific Learning Disability: 405 students
Autism: 114 students
Traumatic Brain Injury: 4 students

While vision impairment and orthopedic impairment are clear cases in which the student would need support to be successful in school, four of the above categories, again with the highest numbers, are based on little tangible evidence, but rather on the fact that the student is failing. Mental retardation, emotional disturbance, other health impairment (ADHD,) and specific learning disabilities, in my experience, are hard to diagnose, and often result in inflated numbers.

It is my personal experience that many students having been diagnosed as special needs in any of these four categories have certainly not shown difficulty in learning, but rather their lack of success has had more to do with socioeconomic issues and behavioral problems. My colleagues and I have continually noted and discussed the fact that certain students were completely mislabeled and in no way could be considered special needs, yet still were. The confusion comes from a student having a history of bad grades.

The logic currently being employed is that if a student has all bad grades, there has got to be SOMETHING wrong with them. Then, it becomes a goal for school officials to try to find a category of special needs in which the kid might fit, again, to show that efforts are being put into helping the student. If the student scores high on standard tests and can't be labeled "mentally retarded," well then they can certainly be labeled as "emotionally disturbed," and receive extra funding.

While there is countless anecdotal evidence to suggest that the diagnosis of these disorders is completely subjective, there is statistical evidence as well. The testimony to the subcommittee mentioned above describes an "Over-Identification for Special Education" in which minorities have been statistically more likely to be deemed "special needs."

In the testimony, it is reported that "According to the NRC (National Research Council) report, while African-American students comprise of 17 percent of the student population they account for 20 percent of students identified for special education. More troubling, black students account for 33 percent of those identified as mentally retarded as well as 27 percent of those identified with emotional disturbances." It continues to say "... an African-American student is 2.28 times more likely to be identified as mentally retarded and 1.58 times more likely to be identified as emotionally disturbed than a white student."

Any time such a discrepancy is found, it quickly becomes obvious that the testing and diagnosis for a disorder is wildly flawed. Rather than a physiological explanation for low performance, there is obviously a social one. But again, we often try to solve social problems in the academic arena, with little success. Labeling a kid "special needs" due to some reason for struggle in school other than ability is unfair and irresponsible.

As grades and success in school often have little to do with natural ability, real gains will only be made when we realize that many of these students are struggling due to socioeconomic reasons rather than intellectual ones. Putting extra funding towards these kids is a great idea, but the funds need to be placed correctly. Their struggle is likely NOT academic and so dumping money into the schools that assist them is not the way to address the problem.

I can recall a meeting in which a parent was told that her son would receive extra support because he was diagnosed as mentally retarded. Naturally she was furious, but the counselors considered it to be good news, as he would be given more support and funding. Because he was a student in my science class, and I had extensive experience in working with him, I found the diagnosis to be absurd.

The diagnosis was based on the results of a series of tests, and if a student tests low enough, he or she is determined to be mentally retarded. Because this kid was well spoken verbally, very popular, and a good athlete, a casual assessment by any sane person would never lead to the conclusion that he was mentally retarded. Rather, I attribute his low test scores to a life-long lack of interest in school, extreme laziness, and from a lack of focus on education from his family.

Similarly, I have taught students considered to be ED or emotionally disturbed. The funny thing is that this is a fancy term for being bad. While this may seem an oversimplification, it seems ridiculous that a student would be given extra accommodations and extra resources for consistently telling teachers to F off. We had one student that had a record of beating his girlfriend, as well as other violent crimes, and our only discussions were how to use the extra funds to serve him. To point out the backwards logic of this situation, do we give extra funds to kids who don't beat their girlfriends and who don't commit violent crimes? Of course we don't.

The other two subjective categories were those of "Other Health Impairment (ADHD,) and "Specific Learning Disability." While there are certainly cases in which a student can not succeed with out support to overcome such disabilities, these diagnosis are grossly over used. And even in the case that a person is found to have some disorder of this type, what should be done? A colleague of mine, with a master's degree in psychology, stated that she was diagnosed with ADD, even as an adult. Her immediate response was "so what?" With or without ADD, she will still go to work, still pay her bills, still feed her pets, and act responsibly. So what does this designation mean for her as an adult? This is an important point.

In the job place or in the real world, employers do not give extra accommodations for people with these subjective disorders. That is, no boss would say "I understand that you only told me to F off because you have been diagnosed with 'emotional disturbance disorder' so don't worry about it." No, this person would instantly be fired. Are we really serving students by justifying behaviors that need to be dropped? Whether or not a person has ADHD, do they not have to focus at work? Our schools are supposed to prepare our young for the world, and with this complete abuse of diagnosing our young with speculative disorders we are justifying behaviors that in the past were considered unacceptable. Whatever the case, dumping funds into correcting these issues is completely irresponsible.

For the group that does not have behavioral issues, but real developmental issues, the funding still seems misplaced. The total dollar amount per kid is not necessarily something to be frowned upon, but that the money isn't being used to create real and productive change is. The premise for how these kids are measured is based on some "norm" in academic subjects and great effort is put into having them reach that norm. A more intelligent approach would be to find what they do embrace and what they are naturally good at and put the money into developing that potential into an income earning endeavor. Repeating fractions and decimal instruction for years on end in an attempt to raise their score on a standardized test, when they clearly don't show an ability in or an affinity for math, in no way is using our valuable resources to better the lives of these kids.

As an example, I have had kids in my class that were deemed to have "special needs." How things worked was that the kid would sit in my math class and wasn't able to grasp the concepts we discussed. After class, he or she would bring their work to a follow up day class of about ten kids with three teachers (extremely costly,) and the math would be reviewed for a second time. Then, typically, the kid still wouldn't understand the work entirely, but because of a pre-determined schedule, he would arrive at class the following day for a new topic. Then, he would bring that topic to the resource class, and the cycle continues. On tests, the kid consistently received F's, but was able to pass because we "modify" grades for special needs students. It would be wrong to punish a kid for legitimately trying, so the student receives a C but is not allowed to move forward. The following year, the student takes the same class, and much of the same occurs again.

This discussion is absolutely not a critique of the above student's math abilities, but of the system now in place. The plan as it stands has no room for diversity with regards to academic ability, and crudely tries to cram every student into the same tight little box. The expression "no child left behind" has a positive tone to it, but it might be more accurately called "no child left to choose a different path." If the resources that were designated to push this child against the current towards a series of disappointments were used to push him in the direction of his passions and abilities, a realistic goal that could lead to success in adulthood may have been reached.

And again, almost any cost would merit improvement for our kids, if indeed the efforts were successful, but many kids, like the one described above, simply never attain that desired level of math understanding. Even with the efforts described, this student will clearly not go onto to major in math in college or a subject that is heavy in math, and so one has to question the intense focus on the accumulation of that math. If the answer has anything to do with Russia and whether they did or did not send shuttles to the moon first, the program has its goals backwards and our kids are paying the price.

How we distribute funds and to whom they are directed needs to be flipped entirely. I actually envision a system with the exact opposite approach. I envision the kids that show both an affinity to and ability in math being the ones that are sent to a second math class, in which they are given further and more deep instruction on math and science. I envision these small class sizes as being a privilege earned through hard work and that the kids who excel would be the ones rewarded with small and creative classes.

As the above breakdown of funding described, general education kids were receiving roughly $8,000 per year, while the special needs kids were receiving $19,000 per year. I would like to see either a smaller gap in the two, or greater funding being directed towards those that show a love for learning and an interest in working hard. I would like to see the distribution of funds be a reward for achievement, rather than a reward for failure. And where effort is put in but the results are unlikely, I would like to see the funding sill be given to those kids, but that they be used for training in a field that is both realistic and interesting to them. How funding is distributed today is nothing short of lunacy.

I can remember a story that my biochemistry professor at the University of California, Santa Cruz told me. He was born in China and came from a very small farming village, in which incomes were modest and hard work was a norm. From early on his village recognized that he appeared to be "gifted" and encouraged his focus on academic studies. When the time came, he took and passed an entrance exam into a fine private high school, an incredible feat. In order to send him to this expensive school, the entire village pooled their resources and sent him on his way. This bright young student went on to be successful in this school, studied in America, and received his PhD in molecular biology. The village obviously could not afford to, nor did they consider it wise, to put the same resources into every person born in the village. And according to the professor, there was no shame in the kids who didn't follow that path. All individuals were encouraged to head in the direction that was natural to them, given both ability and, maybe more importantly, affinity.

This seems like a rational and intelligent way to allocate resources, but would not be considered in America.

Put another way, math programs could become more like athletic teams, with cuts and tryouts, so that it is an honor to be a part of them. Never have I heard of a football team forcing a kid to play, and then when they don't show an interest or ability in the sport, offer them mandatory extra courses to go over the plays and drills. To be successful in football, there has to be both a natural ability and the intense desire to be successful. Sports are voluntary and are very difficult to be successful in, yet no rosters go unfilled. This might be why those involved have such pride. Math programs would likely see the same sort of involvement and exclusive rights of membership that the football programs enjoy today.

So, to create change, we have to review and alter the fundamental principle of uniformity that we have so faithfully rallied behind. The basis, again, for the misdirected distribution of funds is that every kid should be doing the same math, science, and or any subject. It certainly makes sense that we as a society would want to support at risk kids, both for selfish and unselfish reasons, as having all people come up in standard of living is a benefit to us all. Our only flaw in logic has been that we think each of these kids should be headed in exactly the same direction.

This misplacement of our resources is not just a school wide problem, but a societal issue that we as a nation have struggled with for years. A friend of mine, with a big heart, runs a business in which they educate prisoners, many with violent crimes, and teach them English. These are criminals who have been convicted of murder and rape, and this program takes tax money to help them. They also help them fill out job applications, and counsel them on how to succeed when they get out of jail.

In a recent discussion with her, I asked her why she didn't offer the same service to the janitors that work in our office complex, who put in absurd hours just to feed their kids, but that don't speak English. Every day the same workers come and clean the stairs and restrooms in our offices, working long hours, and would benefit from the ability to speak English fluently. These people are kind, hardworking, and always give a smile and a wave to those around them, but have chosen not to be violent or engage in criminal activity. Don't they deserve help? Haven't they earned, through hard work, the opportunity to receive extra help to succeed? With our current attitude about the distribution of funds, resources will never go to these deserving people, but rather to people who made the personal choice to stab, rape, or rob someone. This backward thinking is something that we as a nation need to address, starting with our schools.

CHAPTER 21: TENURE AND TEACHER REWARDS

To analyze the effectiveness of a program in schools today that is protected by teachers with great passion, the policy of tenure does not make sense. Although I would benefit directly from tenure, as I teach in a public school, and have family members that teach and benefit from tenure, it is only fair to review the policy with objectivity. If one were to suggest to a private company that they employ a policy like tenure, laughter would be the only response. Tenure really is an absurd concept.

Again, as is so often the case with governmental policies, the intent behind the policy of tenure is a good one. Originally, tenure was created as a lure to attract good teachers. In a career that can't offer high monetary gains, policy makers were against a wall to find a way to still have talent consider teaching as a real option. Where money isn't ever going to be in abundance for public schools, those in charge figured they may be able to offset this by offering a large degree of job security. Tenure is the most extreme case of a policy that delivers this, so sought after, job security, apart from maybe the military.

Many consider all government jobs to fall into this category of offering job security to begin with and this has always been an attractant. The government, with its ability to levy taxes, will likely never go bankrupt and can therefore employ people indefinitely. This piece of mind has long served as a major influence in one's decision to enter a career with the government, and should continue to be so. There is certainly no sin in offering or looking for job security.

But, there is a very real reason that no major corporation in this country would agree to a policy such as tenure. In the case of a corporation, it is in their best interest not to have a high turnover of employees and, providing the individual is performing, it is very possible to have a high degree of job security. But, the business wouldn't guarantee job security on paper, because of the obvious fact that a person could, for whatever reason, decide to become extremely complacent and to not do his or her best to succeed. This potential threat alone is reason enough for companies not to adopt a policy like tenure.

Arguably, though, the worst consequence of tenure is the idea that once teachers have become "untouchable," they feel no need to address the concerns of students and their parents. Much of the animosity that can exist between parents and teachers stems from this attitude of teachers that "these are my policies and if Johnny doesn't follow them, he'll fail." Having come from a service industry as my first job and having run my own business, this idea that a person can act without regard to the population he or she is serving is foreign to me and is plain wrong. It is not that a teacher should scamper around trying to impress all who call, but for a teacher to not consider the input of his or her audience is ridiculous. If most are discontent with how you are running things, you should spend some time listening and begin to make changes. Tenure ensures that this does not need to happen for many teachers.

In other words, if the classroom were a business and if the success of that business were dependent upon how excited the kids were about learning and how fulfilled they feel, would many of our teachers remain in business or would they fail? I argue that many of our high school teachers would fail. I also argue that if this were a real possibility, they would spend less time demanding certain actions from kids and more time working with them to make sure that they are happy to be there. I have always asked myself whether or not my students would show up to class if it weren't mandatory, and if the answer is a resounding no, I try to make changes to continue to excite them. A teacher can't lean on the fact that the kids simply have to show up, so the design of the class doesn't need to be attractive. Tenure makes it possible for people with this attitude to stay in business.

There is a well known understanding that those who act in a more cavalier manner in schools are tenured, and are thus above the law to a certain degree. On the flip side of that, many young teachers hustle and aim to impress because they are not yet tenured, and long await the day when they will no longer have to do so. This idea that one can reach a certain point where they no longer have to impress anyone is a dangerous concept for the productivity of schools or for any entity.

As I write this, our great country is going through an economic crisis and so I promptly received a "pink slip" and was laid off from my teaching job for the coming year. When I announced this to my classes, they all spoke up and demanded that the "boring" and "mean" teachers be laid off instead. My consequent explanation of how lay-offs worked in public schools shocked the kids, and in turn, allowed me to really reflect on how absurd it is.

My administrator explains it as such. "Picture a ladder. The person who has been teaching the longest is at the top and the person who has arrived most recently is at the bottom. Lay-offs happen from the bottom rung and go up until the budget has been satisfied. Then, if funds are available, those people are asked back in the opposite order, from the highest rungs of lay-offs down. So, the guy at the bottom rung is laid-off first and re-hired last." The kids met this explanation with dropped jaws. Their questions were just the questions that any business owner would ask.

"So it doesn't have anything to do with how good the teacher is?" one kid asked. "What if all of the kids hate one teacher and love the one that got laid-off?" I fielded questions of this nature for the next twenty minutes, repeating that it is based on seniority alone and not on merits. One would think that if a group of 9th graders can see the lack of logic in this policy, so would our administrators. Not the case.

So, again, while one can certainly agree with the logic in designing a lure to bring in intelligent and productive people, through job security, a small problem has been switched out for a larger one. We have done a good job in ensuring that college graduates, like me and others, will give a second look to the career of education. But, in turn we have instilled in these people the possibility and or even the certainty, that they will not be discouraged from apathy and a mediocre career. When we are not given accolades for our achievements, but rather for how long we have been around, we lose the drive to perform and to impress.

Rewards above and beyond tenure are also not based on merit but on an insane system of accumulating professional development credits. So, based on the number of years a teacher has been around, and the number of courses they have taken in their summers or over the internet, the teachers will be rewarded at a certain salary. Again, nowhere in this calculation of salary is the factor of "performance" included.

While this again doesn't seem like a terrible idea, to encourage teachers to continue to learn, it is backwards in how it measures and rewards teachers. What teachers do is look at the list of classes that have been approved for units and pick them based on how fast they can be finished and by how easy they might be. Smart teachers that have become adept at working the system simply take as many of these courses as possible to be put into a higher pay bracket, regardless of the impact the classes have on their effectiveness in the classroom. It would be laughable to think that a private company might let this kind of abuse happen amongst their employees and that they would pay their workers more, not based on performance, but based on how many little internet courses they could cram into a year. So, again, central planners don't lack intelligence, but are simply too far from operations on the ground to be able to measure how efficiently their money is or isn't being used.

So what are some ways to bring talent to the table without the use of the destructive concept of tenure? The fact is that teaching in itself offers many rewards that will bring bright people around, even without tenure. The ideas of the ability to make a huge impact on one's community, the large degree of creativity the job entails, and the very attractive schedule that is so conducive to raising a family are just a few. With these inherent strengths, only a few additional incentives need be added.

I have always been in favor of the idea of debt relief from college loans for students willing to teach in certain neighborhoods, but the program could be spread to teaching in general. It would make sense, along the lines of a "peace corps" type of program to encourage many or all of our brightest academics to consider the career of teaching as an intermediary to another career. It simply isn't the case that one has to have taught for several years to be good, and in fact, some of the most exciting teachers to kids are new ones.

Many times our teenagers will only respond to a teacher in their late twenties or early thirties, for the simple fact that they "understand" more of what life is like for them. This point is not being made to discredit older teachers but to bring merit to "rookie" teachers. Less of teaching is about how papers are collected in an orderly fashion, but has more to do with "reaching' individuals. Relating to the kids seems like an irreplaceable prerequisite to teaching, and in this way, new teachers are often diamonds in the rough.

So if it were a policy of our country to encourage our youngest and brightest to teach, even for just a little while, the kids and our schools would benefit. Then, if a person fell in love with teaching, they certainly wouldn't be discouraged from staying in the field, and wouldn't necessarily need the additional enticements like tenure.

So, to get our brightest to teach for a few years, again, much how the peace corps is able to pick up young talent early in their careers, it would make sense to implement policy to make this short term period attractive. Most new grads are desperate for jobs, are shouldering large loans, and don't have the demands on resources associated with having growing families. Starting with these three factors, we can build a good program.

Before we can move in this direction, though, the current bureaucratic boundaries would have to be diminished or eliminated to make it easier to enter the career for a short period. As it stands, the steps to get into teaching have become prohibitive for some of our most intelligent professionals, and do not serve our kids but harm them. The process to become credentialed is grueling and does not necessarily build a better teacher.

Currently one has to go through a two year program and then has to complete x amount of in-class student teaching. While this varies from state to state, it is consistently too burdensome for its value. I did precisely the above and found very little substantial learning from the coursework, but rather consider my teaching abilities to have come from common sense and actual classroom experience.

College graduates should have to go through a significantly less intensive program to be able to teach, in a time when teachers are so desperately needed, so that they are able to consider it a real option for a "few" years as they develop their own sense of self. It could be viewed as a career that pays relatively well, has a wonderful schedule, and has a certain sense of community service that we often associate with people who enter the military or peace corps while they are young. Then, in addition to this, the young person would be independent, as the career offers benefits and pays more than enough for one individual to survive. For our young people, often less particular in their career demands, teaching offers much of what is hard to find in the private sector.

And, again, relief from the ailment that many young graduates have in the way of college loan debt could be on the table to lure these young academics. Loan reduction or modification, through varying degrees and multiple forms, could make the field of education enticing, if even for only a few years. For federally backed loans, it would absolutely make fiscal sense for the government to reduce interests, reduce actual principal, or to allow for flexible payment to a young person who was willing to serve their community as a teacher. The money that would be paid out in this manner would be recovered as younger teachers command a significantly lower income. Many senior tenured teachers make twice the income that a young teacher does. This gap could be decreased by adjusting the terms on the loans for these college graduates.

It makes sense for the field of education to shift away from retaining older teachers and towards drawing in younger teachers. Without the two and a half kids and the mortgage, people directly out of college require less to live on, and as we have less to give, as public schools, this seems like a perfect marriage. This, again, would be similar to how the peace corps does not typically attract people with children, but rather, young people with few needs and a large sense of adventure.

And to ensure that the teachers come in with at least a certain amount of craft, the model would be along the lines of a privately run company. The schools would have a few, highly paid veteran teachers that act as "managers" to a much larger and younger work force of teachers in schools. These older teachers could offer curriculum, tests, and other administrative support that comes with experience, and the younger teachers could simply follow the program and "do their thing." The "do their thing" is an under-rated factor and would make for a wonderful learning environment if the recent college graduate is bright and motivated.

Then, as there would have been a shift away from having a predominantly all tenured and experienced staff, there would be available funds to offer this "manager" type of position a much larger income. Just as CEO'S of companies earn high incomes, these few elite teachers would be rewarded. They of course would attain the position through productivity and merit as opposed to it being a function of how long they managed to stick around. So, modeling after the corporate world, schools could quickly and easily be transformed into fresh, exciting, and productive places with teachers who have just left the most inspirational of all places, our wonderful universities.

A trade that we should willingly make for the sake of our kids is the slightly less organized classroom structure that a rookie brings, for the inspiration and excitement for life that accompanies it. It is completely incorrect to state that the effectiveness of a teacher is solely a function of his or her time in education. So, while discarding tenure would be step one in transforming who and what teachers are, a much larger overhaul of how schools are created and run is needed.

Every kid in America would benefit from having brilliant young people just out of our universities as role models and teachers, just as those graduates would benefit from the strength in character that comes along with having spent time bettering others. Teaching is a learning experience for both the student and the person delivering the lectures. For these reasons, we should stop encouraging mediocrity and should create a system that would welcome our brightest.

Chapter 22: Parents Have a Choice

B ECAUSE OF THE STATE OF large public high schools today, parents are becoming more open to alternative ideas as to what high school is supposed to be like, and different forms of school are starting to take shape. For parents who aren't savvy to what is happening in education today, though, large high schools and public schools are the default choice, as they feel as though other options don't exist. The good news is that other options do in fact exist. Just because we went to large public high schools and survived, it should not be the automatic assumption that it is the best route for our kids.

It is also my feeling that academics should not be the only factor in deciding what school we send our kids to. Maybe more important is the ambience that the school has to offer, as we are allowing four very important years of our kids' lives to be shaped by this atmosphere. Before discussing the options available besides a large public high school, though, an epiphany I had between classes needs to be discussed.

While this is obviously a comical claim, there are very real similarities between our public high schools and our prisons, and maybe not for the benefit of our children. Frankly, our public high schools need help.

First of all, many people mention that they would like their kids to attend a public high school because they don't want to shelter their kids. That is, they want their kids to see "real-life" so that they can function in society as adults. They somehow find the goings on of high school to be parallel to what we as adults experience in this alleged "real life." To pause, do you have a job or a lifestyle that is similar to the public high school experience?

Fortunately, high school is in no way like a miniature version of my adult life, and in fact, it would be hard to imagine any situation as an adult in which your life would be similar to what our high school kids do day in and day out. There is no place in our society that parallels high school, except for, of course, prison.

At no time throughout my day as an adult do I travel in a large pack with peers of roughly my exact age, moving according to a system of bells and loudspeaker announcements. Also, I can't remember the last time I raised my hand to politely ask for the opportunity to go pee, and was allowed to relieve myself pending I sign a sheet and carry a large toilet seat cover with me on my trip to said bathroom. As an adult surrounded by other adults, I consistently seek to and am rewarded for developing a sense of individuality and do not feel as though I need to follow a norm to avoid stinging criticism.

In prison the inmates respond to a series of bells that dictate where they are to go and what they are to do. They are given certain amounts of time to engage in recess type activity, as well as other pre-determined times to do productive work. The prisons have large eating areas similar to the cafeterias in high schools, and depending on the prison or school, one may or may not stray from campus. As is the case in prisons, highs schools have a ranging patrol of security, assigned to curtail the dangerous activities of its inhabitants. Depending on the school and or the crime associated with that community, metal detectors and routine searches are common.

Above all of this, however, is similarity in the behavior of the inmates of prisons and the students of our local high schools. When asked how kids feel about school and how they fit in, they answer much the same way that prisoners do. "If you get in with a certain group early on and lay low, you'll be fine."

Just as in the case of prison, the kids leave class to immediately find the security of their group and almost never stray into the un-chartered waters of the territories of other groups. Even having to tend to some administrative detail in the office can set kids away from their safety net and results in extra stress. To remedy this, many kids won't travel campus alone, but meet their friends so as to keep with the "buddy" system. While the consequences of being caught alone in prison might be greater than those of being caught alone in a public high school, the mentality is none the less the same. Students take great lengths to not be alone at break or lunch. And while the threat in high schools is not real, but perceived, high school is hardly the safe haven that we would like for our kids to explore, be creative, and grow. Rather than this, large public schools foster insecurities and promote extreme competitiveness.

For this reason, more individuality and creativity can often be observed in smaller private schools or home school groups. With smaller groups and a more inclusive ambience, kids are allowed to indulge in their creative leanings and can often be seen dressing more individually or even acting with more candid quirkiness. This may be exactly what parents are guarding against, by sending their kids to large public high schools, but I find value in the ability of kids to act freely along these lines.

As an example of the difference between a student of a large public high school and that of an alternative school, I can recall a tutoring session in which I was helping a kid from a large public high school. We were finishing up and my next student, a kid from a small home school collective, came in. When the homeschooled kid came in wearing a fedora type hat, not unlike that of Indiana Jones, he drew immediate attention from the kid from the large public high school.

Upon our next visit, the kid from the large public high school stated that "that kid wouldn't last ten minutes at my school with that hat on." Regardless of whether or not that particular style of hat is cool or not, this shows the extreme social pressure that exists and is fostered when huge groups of relatively insecure kids are put together on one campus. I don't wear hats like that, but I don't think that a kid should be picked on and ridiculed for doing so. And for the record, with regards to character and personality, the home school kid in question was very popular and is a stand out. He is funny, charming, and intelligent, but just hasn't learned the tough lessons of mandatory conformity that kids in public schools are forced to learn early on.

The irony in the above story was that the public school kid would assume that I would and should feel sorry for the home school kid, but the opposite was true. I genuinely feel sorry for kids at large public high schools that do not have the freedom to explore their individuality, for fear that they will be committing social suicide.

The kid in the above story from the public high school, like the other, is also sweet, funny, and kind, but because of his peers, had a much different look. In order to fit in, he wears saggy pants, a lowered hat, and has a sort of a "tough guy" look. Frankly, he sports the kind of look that many adults frown upon, with a slightly gangster hue. In no way is this kid a gangster, and left to his own creativity, he may not have created such a look. But, the choice between being picked on or conforming is a real one and, thus, he went with the gangster look. Who should we feel sorry for, the individualistic kid who is allowed to be "himself," or the conforming kid who has to put up a false image so as not to draw attention? I know what I want for my kids.

So, again, it seems that this concept of conforming to survive does not exist anywhere in our adult lives in the same prevalence as it does in high school, and thus, the argument that sending our kids to a public high school to prepare them for adult life does not hold water. The only place that I think the lessons of the survival in the large public high schools would serve one well is in prison. If these aren't the lessons that you had in mind when you enrolled your child in the local high school, you'll be happy to hear that there are alternatives.

Chapter 23: Alternatives to Large Public Schools

THE ALTERNATIVES TO LARGE PUBLIC high schools today include charter schools, private schools, home-study programs, home-schooling, and home-school collectives. As one would expect, all of these have their positive attributes along with their negatives, but it is certainly refreshing to know that we have options and that not all of these options have the prerequisite of extreme wealth. And rather than committing to one form of education over the other, many families find themselves navigating through different types of schools at different times in the lives of their children.

The closest cousin of our large public high school is the phenomenon that seems to be gaining momentum, the concept of the charter school. Charter schools are essentially public schools that have requested and have been granted license to receive government funding, yet are able to retain some sort of creative individuality. Charter schools typically adopt a certain perspective or identity and fill a certain niche in the community by doing so.

For instance, in Santa Cruz County, in California, charter schools range from offering an extreme rigorous academic schedule to a program designed for drop-outs from other schools. As well, there are certainly charter schools that are somewhere in the middle of the two spectrums, but that promote maybe a strength in the arts or the concept of more group learning. Regardless of the specific focus of the charter school, however, if they are to remain accredited, they are subject to the same regulations and standardized testing that any governmentally funded school would be. This guarantees a certain level of conformity, ensuring that the school is not so radical that your child may not receive what is considered to be a normal education.

Charter schools are finding success and one of the key reasons might not be easily notable upon first inspection. The answer lies in the clientele of the charter schools. Like private schools who cater to a select group, typically from wealthy homes, charter schools have their own unique clientele. To attend a charter school, a student has to apply for and be allowed to transfer from their designated school to that charter school. Automatically, by the mere fact that families have to apply to enter these schools as opposed to just attending their local large public high school because of their zip code, the schools have a different student body. That is, it takes a certain parent to investigate and pursue a school based on specific merits, so mere apathy alone keeps other kids out.

It could be argued that an important first step in the right direction is that the parent had to put at least a little effort and time into the academic future of their child. Those who lack the interest or the desire to apply to the charter school are automatically, again by default, left to the large public school within "x" amount of miles from their home. This inherent selection process is largely left out of the discussion of charter schools, but might be one of the dominant factors in their success in creating a certain ambience.

There is no inhibitive cost associated with charter schools, which makes them an attractive choice for families who don't have the means to enter private schools or that can't afford to have one parent stay home to facilitate home-schooling, but who still place a high value and priority on education. This is a huge bonus for families looking for a solution for their child, but that have ruled out the other more expensive alternatives to a large public high school.

The only thing that even comes close to being a restrictive policy with regards to income, though, is that some charter schools are able to make parental involvement mandatory. One local charter school, known for their academic rigor and success in attaining a consistently high level of education, has mandatory volunteer hours and asks a certain amount of time from parents on a monthly basis. While this policy is intelligent and, again, attracts a certain type of parent, some families may live with the reality that work consumes much of their free time and a single parent or struggling family may not be able to allocate that extra time away from home. Beyond a policy of this sort, though, the schools are essentially as cost-free as any other public high school.

Speculation as to whether or not students from charter schools score better in math and English is inconclusive. There have been studies done that find that this is indeed the case, but these studies were immediately challenged and many have discredited them based on their methods in collecting data. What isn't a debate, however, is whether or not charter schools are able to create alternative experiences to large public schools. They are indeed successful in doing this. Charter schools are becoming a wonderful option for parents who want more from high school for their kids.

Often times, when parents ask me my opinion of whether or not they should send their kids to private school or public school, I mention that they wouldn't be paying for better teachers at a private school, necessarily, but for a particular ambience. This, again, is what charter schools are beginning to be able to offer. I put more importance on what "reality" my kids grow up in, rather than their ability to outscore South Korea in math, and so would shop for a certain "vibe" over performance.

My goal for my kids, which is also likely a goal for you and your kids, is to create a wonderful and bright childhood that is conducive to learning and success. I don't find it a priority to squabble over what school might get my kids a few more points on the SAT. For this reason, I would choose ambience over almost anything when shopping for a school. Whatever one's focus, as a cost-free option, many are finding charter schools to be the solution for the problem of how to find a unique learning environment, without the cost of a private school.

The next largest option for education, away from the norm, is that of private schools. Private schools are hardly new, but have some pros and cons that are not completely apparent at face value. Interestingly enough, the high cost for tuition doesn't go to better teachers as a rule, but again, to ambience.

More often than not, the better teachers that are interested in teaching for a career make their way to public schools eventually, as public schools offer much better pay and benefits than do the private schools. Most private schools simply can't afford to offer lengthy and generous retirement packages and can't keep up with the pay increases that the large public school systems can afford. For this reason, again, many young teachers with the idea of doing the job for life apply for public school jobs.

The exception to this, which is not uncommon, is in the event that a teacher does not have to be concerned with money. Specifically, many spouses of relatively wealthy people will teach at a private school as they prefer the culture and often do it for reasons other than income. One example is spouses who teach at a particular private school to receive free tuition for their kids. When this is the case, there is a real possibility that the teacher may be passionate and successful without feeling as though they have to make the move to a public school for higher pay. Because these people are personally invested in the success of the school, with their kids attending, they can make for some of the best teachers.

But if, in the majority of cases the teachers are not better or more qualified, why go to a private school? A huge perk to private schools is that they are certainly in the position to create a desired atmosphere, as they can control who they let in and who they remove. This is a fundamental difference between public and private schools. In public schools it is not uncommon for a child to cuss at a teacher or engage in a fight with another kid, only to be scolded and allowed to return. There are kids in public schools that use and sell drugs, despite the fact that many know, and they may have even been caught before.

The process for removing a student from a public high school is a very difficult, while it takes a flip of the hand from the principal to remove a kid from a private school. This control over "clientele" allows private schools to maintain a much more peaceful and trouble free environment than is seen in public schools. This fact alone, without any discussion as to the academic merits of a particular private school, might be reason enough for parents to be interested in the private program.

Private schools, again, are also less restricted by red tape as they don't depend on state funding and can be creative in their approach. Obviously, in the case of religious private schools, they can offer a specific upbringing that is in alignment with the values of religious parents. But no less common are schools with other emphasis, such as an emphasis on the sciences, or on a particular approach to life. There is a little private elementary school in the mountains of Santa Cruz, California that has an apple orchard as its campus and that focuses on a love for nature. This ability to cater to a specific audience is a major strength of private schools. Again, because they aim to fill a very specific niche, and because the free market determines the success or failure of private schools, they are often able to provide a product impossible to find in the public school system.

In the private school at which I taught in Hawaii, the atmosphere was well-crafted and ideal. It was an all girls' school and the kids would participate in countless ceremonies, from mass to flag each morning, which by their very nature set a certain scene. Regardless of one's feelings about religion, the concept of gathering and pondering things deeper than fractions and commas is a valuable thing. By getting together outside of the classroom, there was a tremendous sense of belonging and a strong sense of community that I have not seen since. The concept of mass is valuable for more than just the enrichment that religious people find from it. I enjoyed the group singing and the community spirit associated with mass, yet I have no religious affiliations.

A thing to be wary of, though, with regards to private schools is their advertisements bragging of high standardized test scores, suggesting that they might be able to give an edge to your specific child. It is no secret to teachers in both public and private schools that the fastest way to raise the average test scores of a student body is by simply removing the low achievers. More often than not, a private school has high test scores because of who is interested in their school, rather than anything that they have done with regards to curriculum or style of teaching. A shocking realization along these lines was made in Hawaii, when a notoriously high performing private school disclosed their acceptance policies. If the kid didn't already score high on standardized tests, they simply weren't allowed in. So, for high test scores in private schools, the egg usually comes before the chicken, and the students were excellent long before they started at the particular private school.

Even so, high test scores could still be the deciding factor in the choice of one private school over another, not because of the ability of the school to create geniuses, but for, again, the atmosphere. A parent might prefer a school that has hand picked academic students because of the social setting created by that school. They might be attracted to the idea that their kids would become friends with productive people, rather than associate with low achievers. So while an academic private school will not make a child into a prodigy using some secret ground breaking techniques, merely hanging out with other outstanding students and being influenced by them and their attitudes might help.

So, as has been the case for years, private schools continue to provide a wonderful product for parents looking for an alternative to public schools. Unfortunately, this option is ruled out for many families as resources are always going to be an issue and these schools may simply be too expensive. But, when financially possible, it makes sense for parents to look into this option before simply settling for the school nearest to them.

Another whole arena that offers an alternative to the traditional large public high school is that of learning at home. While "homeschooling" is not a new notion, the face of homeschooling has changed dramatically. There are different types of learning at home, and each has a different approach. The three most common forms are that of home schooling, home study, and home school collectives. The latter is not unlike a small private school, but offers more flexibility.

Homeschooling conjures up images of the isolationist family whose aim it is to shelter their child from the trends of society. We immediately picture a "cult" mentality or kids being raised in an extreme religious practice, in which the ideals of current education go against said religion. For this reason, the idea of home schooling is often ruled out and is especially shun by kids themselves. Many kids state that home school kids will turn out "weird," as they aren't taught the lessons that we all need from the school yard. I am here to say that this is simply no longer the case. The home school kids that I have met are not only "normal," but are often excellent in that they are afforded more time to become an expert in what they have an interest in.

The two reasons that homeschooling seems to make sense for some families are pacing and schedule. In a perfect world, our kids would be allowed to learn at a natural pace, allowing for quicker movement when the ability and interest are present, and a slower pace for harder material or for a time in life when the interest is elsewhere. The idea that every kid at a particular age should be in the same academic place is contrary to human behavior and is a ridiculous notion. There are certainly developmental similarities amongst all people, so that at a specific age, we all are able to do roughly the same things. But this is not so clear that we can guarantee it and design specifics of curriculum along these lines.

One home school parent told me of her and her husband's decision to home school after a particular revelation through a discussion with the first grade teacher of their child. The mother mentioned that, for one reason or another, the majority of the kids in the school began to develop an intense interest in dinosaurs. The kids all began to sport lunch boxes with dinosaurs on them and many of the kids began to memorize the names of some of the more common dinosaurs.

The mom said that she noticed the trend, and while shopping, she came across a really neat set of dinosaur models, in which the kids would be able to recreate the skeletons of dinosaurs, showing their differences and similarities. The models came with scientific coloring books and pictures of each dinosaur. Without hesitation, she bought the set and was excited to offer it as a gift to the teacher on the coming Monday.

To her shock and dismay, however, the teacher thanked her but stated that she couldn't use them yet. When the mom appeared confused, the teacher explained that the state and federal standards didn't include dinosaurs until a later grade, and that she had other material to cover. The mom obviously made the case that "but they all love dinosaurs now." This is exactly the problem with pre-determining a pace or plan for all kids across America. There is not the flexibility to let the kids explore what interests them at that exact moment. Homeschooling does allow for this, and this particular mom decided that traditional school simply didn't make sense. She pulled her kid out of traditional schooling and has not had a single regret.

As another example, one can reflect back on the development of his or her own children. Did each child begin to speak at exactly the same age in months? Did each child develop the ability to manipulate small toys at exactly the same age? Similarly, did they all find enjoyment in exactly the same toys and books? Was their no individuality in their abilities and preferences?

Applying this logic to the later ages, it doesn't make sense to expect our children to embrace and excel at each subject at exactly the same age. For instance, if a child shows an affinity and ability in math, are they not allowed to move forward more quickly in that subject than in writing? Can a person push ahead in one subject faster than another? Is there a reason that a fifth grader should show fifth grade competence in every subject, even if they have the potential to be a fifth grade reader but a seventh grade math student? In the real world, a student would show a different grade level of competence for each subject. They might be a seventh grade writer, but a fourth grade mathematician. Homeschooling allows for this individualized pacing, without the negative feedback we see in school in which the kid is assigned a letter grade for each subject.

A fundamental difference between homeschooling and normal schooling seems to be that the focus for homeschooling is on the positive and normal schooling is on the opposite. For example, a homeschooling parent is likely to say "he is way ahead of his age in writing." A parent from a normal school is likely to say "he is doing fine in everything except for a C- in math." This is sad, especially when it begins at an early age.

The second huge plus to the idea of homeschooling is that of the schedule of both the kid and the family. As it stands now, school essentially takes the place of a full time job for kids. They attend school for the bulk of a day and often have little energy for much else, once they get out. Like it or not, kids between the age of kindergarten and the twelfth grade have their focus planned out for them, regardless of their passions or inherent abilities.

Homeschooling can be best represented by the "star kids" examples that we see with homeschooling. Kids that are stars, whether in acting, sports, or whatever, are always homeschooled because they simply don't have the time to sit in a class room from 8-3. Locally here in Santa Cruz, we have a child prodigy surfer who is flown around the world to do photo shoots for magazines and to enter international contests, so he obviously can't be bound by the rigorous schedule of normal school.

Any child actor that we are all acquainted with is also, clearly, homeschooled because they simply couldn't excel in or pursue a career in acting with the limitations of the school schedule. The question is, though, whether or not the same philosophy would apply to a "normal" kid. That is, should normal kids have the ability to pursue their own personal passions, allowing academics to take place around that passion?

One parent that was a participant in the home school collective in which I taught, told the story of her three kids that she raised in a home school setting. She pointed out that they all chose their path, and were successful in vastly different ways.

Her first child, she said, showed an affinity for academics early on. He loved math and reading and asked for extra materials. He, again because he was homeschooled, was not familiar with a normal curriculum pace, and simply moved forward as quickly as he enjoyed. Naturally, because of his excitement for learning, his pace was probably three fold that of normal school. He went on to get his GED and to attend the local junior college while still in his early teens. He then went on to be very successful in college and is a professional to this day. This obviously could not have happened in a traditional school setting, as the parents would have had to deal with an intense amount of red tape just to let their child grow at his own natural pace.

Applying to have one's child skip grades is a daunting task, and many standardized tests prevent that from happening. It is easier in our school system to make a case to simply "keep the kid where he belongs." And often, what prevents a kid from moving forward at an accelerated pace is a comment like "if he or she is so smart, why do they have a B in English." As we know, grades are subjective and it is exactly this mentality that is a disservice to our kids. With homeschooled kids, if the desire and the ability are there, the kid can move forward at whatever pace they can handle. What makes this story of their academic child of particular value though, is that the next two kids absolutely did not follow this path.

The next son showed no interest in academics. From an early age, he did the minimum amount of work to learn to read and write, but showed a huge passion for athletics. He began riding his bike longer and longer distances and eventually entered contests. Because this activity was physically healthy and because he was finding confidence and success through biking, his parents encouraged his passion for biking. Now that boy is the youngest member of a professional bicycle team that competes in contests including the Tour de France, and receives a salary to do what he loves. He has been mentioned among riders of the likes of Lance Armstrong and many think he will be one of the best. Because of his success at an early age, he has a long and bright future ahead of him. There is no question that this lifestyle wouldn't have been possible with the normal restrictions of a standard school schedule.

The third child is a girl and has become a master of the classical piano and enjoys the arts. For her age, people are jaw-dropped by her performances and wonder how she could be so accomplished at such a young age. The answer is that she simply has more time to do the things that she enjoys.

The reason I bring this family up is because they found success in different ways and a degree of their success was due to the flexibility of their schedule. This is exactly the "pro" for a child being raised in a home school situation. And as the child develops, a decision as to how much academic work makes sense for them can be made. In the case of the bike rider, the family made sure that the child met basic academic needs, but in the case of the "student" they fed him materials in piles.

This specialization makes for a much more intelligent approach to learning for different kids. In the above case, the "student" would have been applauded in school, providing he didn't become bored and lose interest, but the "biker" would have been labeled a "bad student," and negativity would have been a large part of his life in the early years. Needless to say, he is not an underachiever, but because of the expectations of the narrow minded approach to school today, he would have been labeled as one.

And to ensure that a parent has at least a rough understanding of what should be taught and at what ages, home schooling is done along with actual formal programs. There are countless accredited online home school programs that offer the materials and the approximate pacing for home schooling, as well as local public home school programs in every city. This way, the parent doesn't have to face the burden of creating a well educated human being on their own. They can usually use the materials as little or as much as they need, and will likely supplement that material as they see fit. The rough scaffolding, though, is important and is certainly available in many forms for home schooling families.

The disclaimer, though, to a family considering home schooling is that a direct effort must be made to ensure that the child has a productive lifestyle. Whether it is piano, riding bikes, or reading books, the parents have an obligation to make sure that the kids are actively engaging in some particular passion or passions. Home schooling is not and was not designed to give a kid more time to sleep in and more time to play video games online. If home schooling is abused, this is where one sees the development of anti-social individuals and is why home schooling developed a reputation for putting out "weird" kids in the past.

A parent has to replace the social settings found in school through other activities. Dance classes, summer swim teams, theatre groups, and an infinite number of other groups can give a kid the social interactions that make a productive and happy person. The internet and fantasy video games DO NOT offer the social interactions necessary for normal development. This being said, home schooling, when done right, is an awesome option for many families, and has produced many outstanding kids.

To supplement the home schooling lifestyle, home school collectives have sprung up around the country. These are basically just little schools where these home schooled kids get together for extra social interaction, and are run by teachers, whether formally trained or not. Some kids attend every day, for a few hours, while other kids can take as little or as much from the school as their family deems important. Some kids only show up for a math section, while others just come for the arts. These are usually privately run and are extremely flexible. And again, apart from the learning that happens in these collectives, these seem largely to have been developed to offer more time to these kids to be with others of similar age. While related to private schools, home school collectives differ in that they are far less rigorous and, again, offer varying schedules, depending on what a family is looking for. Home school collectives are a fine supplement to the schedule of a home schooled kid.

Separate from home schooling and home school collectives, but with a similar name is the notion of "home study." Home study is a program that most or all high schools offer to kids enrolled in their schools to do comparable work, but at home. That is, the kid is officially enrolled in a particular high school, but does the work when possible and in the comfort of their home.

Typically the work is written and is the completion of predetermined assignments. A normal assignment for math might be to do x amount of problems, to be turned in the following Monday. The kid comes in once a week to pick up the work and to drop off the completed work from the past week's assignment. History might include an essay or short answer questions to a particular chapter. The curriculum is usually lighter in nature and tests and quizzes are either not used or are less frequent than in the normal class setting.

The development of these programs was historically for families in which the kids weren't able to attend school regularly. For example, the program might be for a kid who is needed to help at home, or by pregnant teens who simply can't attend high school given their circumstances. The question, again, though, is whether or not this program makes sense for kids in more normal circumstances.

One kid that I tutored chose to do home study for her junior and senior year in high school, and found it to be a perfect solution. She worked in the day, making money to support her driving and other leisure activities, and did the academic work around that schedule. In addition to the benefit of having more free time to do what she pleased, she was also relieved to be free from what many kids consider to be a smothering high school atmosphere. Some kids develop and mature earlier and find the "drama" associated with high school to be an unnecessary stress. This particular girl was ready to live in a more "real life" setting by her junior year, and found this through home study.

Also, this kid was able to actually get ahead in classes and was given work to do over the summer to make even more progress. So again, while home study is not the solution for every kid in every situation, this is yet one more option for school.

Rather than debate the best option for the education of our kids, it makes more sense to understand that there are indeed these options. While the focus of the above was on the alternatives to large public high schools, many kids do love large public high schools and find success there. Whether it is for the larger sports programs or a thriving drama department, many kids like public high school. If this is the case, there is certainly no need to rock the boat and this is not the exception to the rule necessarily. There, however, is a large enough of a population of our kids, who are not served well in the large school setting, and it is refreshing to know that there certainly are other options. Nothing is more important than the success and happiness of our children, and so an amount of investigation into the potential routes for our children is a good use of time. Every kid is capable of and deserves success, but not every kid finds it in exactly the same way.

Chapter 24: All Boy Vs. All Girl Schools

A NOTHER ENTIRE CATEGORY OF SCHOOLING is that of all boy or all girl schools. While these types of schools seem to be seeing a greater decrease in popularity, they are interesting and have some merit. Many times we as a society are quick to advance and often cast old ideas aside, but this particular cultural anomaly hasn't disappeared entirely.

A good question is, what do the different genders do for each other during the growing process and what are both the negative and positive influences that they have on each other? This subject is very interesting, and having taught in an "all girls" school and having visited an "all boys" school, there seem to be a few truths.

My first formal teaching job, besides the tutoring business that I had founded on Oahu, in Hawaii, was at an all girls Catholic private school. That school year was a learning experience, to say the least, but also was my introduction to some of the most sharp and interesting students to date. The school included every grade from kindergarten to the twelfth grade in high school, and was entirely "girl only." Although we shared assemblies and a few other engagements with the tiny kids, the majority of my interactions were with the middle and high school ages.

It was my task to teach life science to the seventh graders and physics to high school girls of mixed ages. I was awed at everything from how cruel girls could be to each other to how sensitive and wholeheartedly "good" these young kids were. I found that they genuinely wanted to influence the world around them and make fundamental changes to our society, while an equal amount of their energy was spent trying to break the school's sock policy.

The sock policy was that they had to pull their socks all the way up, so in defiance and in an attempt to stay within acceptable fashion norms, they would pull their socks off of their toes and fold them under their feet. In this way, the tops of their socks would appear to be pulled up, but they would ultimately rest lower on their shins. I'm not sure if world peace or lower socks were more important for the girls, but they pursued each with equal vigor.

But with regards to how boys and girls affect each other's growth, I really noticed that the girls in this setting behaved differently than in a co-ed school. In a very real way, these girls were able to cast their inhibitions aside and speak their mind, without fear of some sort of negative feedback from a boy in the room. And while they were certainly still subject to negative feedback from each other, this didn't seem as severe of a threat, and the girls were thus more extroverted.

Whereas in a co-ed school, the class clown is often a rambunctious boy, girls stepped in to fill the role. I really enjoyed watching girls put themselves out on a limb to make wild jokes and to act on a whim, and I found that the girls really seemed empowered. In no way did the girls feel as though they had a position other than that of being in the driver's seat and real learning and growth seemed to flourish. In simple terms, the girls seemed fine without boys around.

The same couldn't be said for the "all boys" school that I visited.

It should be made clear that my role in an "all boys" school was nowhere near as significant as that of the "all girls" school, as I used to tutor a kid a few days a week at his "all boys" school after the final bell had rung. Never the less, I was able to make some observations. The looming obvious reality was that, without any feminine influence, the school had a complete absence of civilization. Where the girls seemed to benefit from not having obnoxious boys around, the boys seemed destitute without girls.

Because, I guess, there was no one around to behave for, everyone was farting, burping, scratching places that should have been left alone, and just acting disgusting in ways that only a group of boys could think up. What was also noticeable was how these kids were able to somehow communicate with more explicative than actual words. In fact, I heard one kid use the F word as a noun, verb, and adjective in just one sentence. As an academic, my first instinct was to be impressed, but as a citizen of this nation facing the prospect of having these guys running things eventually, I quickly became concerned. Shortly put, I believe that a few well placed girls around campus would have changed things dramatically and instantly. "All boys" schools, like our famed fraternities and their reputation for civil behavior, can be a disaster.

Co-ed schools could probably best be described as lying somewhere in between the previous two situations and are by far what we typically have experience with. And as previously stated, I really believe that the presence of girls is what gives schools today the semblance of a civilized group of young individuals. For their service, I will always believe that girls give up a part of their freedom and ability to soar, for the thankless task of teaching boys civility. This, unfortunately, seems to be their burden. For my daughters, I will do my best to teach them to never change their actions to avoid scrutiny from boys, but rather to hover above the insecurities of the confused individuals around them. Do you think they will listen? Me neither.

Either way, I don't think the idea of an all-girl school, or even an all-boy school is ridiculous. Based on the specific goal of a particular family, some of the strengths of these schools might deliver just what is needed. In the case of the student attending the all-boy school, though, some extra "manners" classes might be in order on weekends and at night. Just kidding.

CHAPTER 25: THE VALUE OF TRADES

AND JUST AS CONSIDERATION SHOULD be put into what secondary school setting would be most productive for your kid, a whole arena after high school, it seems, has been grossly under-rated as an alternative to a traditional college experience.

When one ponders what education is, the answer can be unclear. Is it to guarantee a certain level of income and thus a lifestyle, or is it to secure a certain sense of self, independent of money? Because I am a realist and have practical tendencies, I believe that the role of education is to provide training and knowledge that have some practical function in our society.

That being said, though, I do personally pursue knowledge that does not serve me in a financial sense, as do many of you. I enjoy reading history books, autobiographies, and fiction, despite the fact that this information has little practical application. So why do we seek to educate ourselves? Aside from the learning we pursue outside of school, I would argue that we, as Americans, attend high school and college to secure the ability to have an enjoyable career that delivers a certain income. Most also agree that, because financial security is the goal, there are more paths to this success than just the traditional university route.

For those who are tempted to disagree, consider the extreme case. Andre Agassi, the famed professional athlete, reportedly left school to pursue a promising career in Tennis, and has since earned millions and millions of dollars in tournament wins and in endorsements. If Andre was your son, would you be disappointed with him and regret that he not had taken the academic route or would you celebrate his success?

The same case is seen with many professional athletes, actors, and individuals involved in other high flying careers. Universally, these people are all seen as successful and a similar level of success is the goal for our loved ones. And when we advise against pursuing a career of this sort, it isn't because of the nature of the career, but rather because of the unlikelihood of reaching the highest ranks of acting or professional sports. So, again, our advice is money-based, in that we are afraid that if they fail, this route will not be able to support them.

Parents typically want their kids to enter medicine or law for financial reasons, regardless of the taste this leaves in our mouths. So if schooling is aimed at securing a certain income, there is a whole subset of schooling that, for the energy and time invested, is extremely under-rated. Trade schools or "tech schools" are an excellent option for some kids.

With regards to a return on one's investment, trade schools typically take less time to complete and provide real training that all but guarantees entrance into that particular field. Many times the pay is outstanding and the student enters the career running. In a purely practical sense, tech and trade schools are absolutely a good use of time and offer a very practical and elegant alternative to large universities.

Where degrees from large Universities can often be vague and offer a "jack of all trades" approach to education, trade schools allow one to specialize earlier on. The concept of "general education" that consumes the first two years of the typical college student's life does not have a home in trade schools. For this reason alone, providing the young person has a clear direction picked out, trade schools can "cut to the chase" and allow the student to begin to master a particular skill or trade.

Just a few days ago, one of the students in my math class came up to me beaming, stating that he found his plan and life's goal. This came as good news to me, as this particular student struggled in school and was often apathetic about his future. He found a tech school that focused on audio engineering, with an emphasis on live performance sound management. The school, he went on, was only for one year, and the cost was much less than a traditional college, not just because it is shorter, but per year as well. For this kid, who likely would have found the general education classes in college to be boring, this is a perfect solution.

All throughout the development of our society, norms are adopted, remain in place with tenacity, and are eventually replaced by new norms. As it stands, now, the norm for many social groups and or parents from certain neighborhoods is that a successful child attends a four year school university after high school. And while there is certainly nothing wrong with doing so, many can't put a finger on why they demand these results and aren't sure as to the benefits of such a move. What I have found in a personal sense, and by watching those around me, is that a degree from a four year university is not a guarantee of success, nor does it guarantee a certain lifestyle.

Without bringing up the famous college dropouts who became successful, like the founders of both Apple and Microsoft, I have an example from my personal life. The person from my close group of friends that is undisputedly the most successful, in both a financial sense as well as in the development of character and poise, is the one who left college after one year, never to return.

The secret to success is not the degree, but the passion to work hard and to focus your energy on what you aim to accomplish. The friend mentioned above did not leave college to play video games and drink beer, but rather went directly into the Navy Seals. From there, he went on to be successful in the financial industry and is now part owner of a multimillion dollar per year business. The route he took, it can be argued, was three times as difficult to accomplish, than the more traditional route of attending and passing classes in a large college, yet the naïve still cling to the notion that there is simply one way to be successful. So, along with the more famous examples of those who found success outside of the traditional university, my friend had the key components of intelligence and a strong work ethic.

This pertains to the discussion on tech schools and trade schools in that if a person is lucky enough to have a goal or have focus, these places can offer the fastest route to movement in the right direction. The concept of college for most parents interested in sending their children is that the four, or seven years in some cases, will prepare their child to go on to enjoy a successful career and to develop financial independence. For these same reasons, tech or trade schools should at least be part of the discussion, especially in the case that your child seems reluctant to engage in the more cranial and less hands on approach to learning.

And if one does go to college, a discussion should take place explaining that college is a tool. College is not just a place to find fun parties and to meet cool people, as that can happen without enrolling in a college, but rather it is very expensive and should serve as training for a career. Too often, kids are ushered into college, again because of the social norm, and ask their counselor what the easiest major might be. This is no way to begin a tremendous endeavor like college. For the lingering student that has not found their passion in life, a two year school or a tech school might better serve them in the meantime. Then, if their goals and interests lead them to college, they will be successful at that time.

I currently have students that are entering the fire program at the local junior college, and one student that is looking into tech schools that specialize in automotive engineering. I can wholeheartedly say that I don't predict that these kids will be any less successful than those meandering away to four year schools, but am proud that they have found direction. It is hardly a flaw to wish the best for your kid and to hope that they get into and enjoy what a large university has to offer, but it wouldn't be a good idea to force this path against obvious signals in the other direction.

A meeting with a parent recently shed light on the insecurities that surround the whole world of academics and our children. This particular child had a father that was a contractor and a "Mr. fix it." For a living, his dad did anything from adding on extra rooms to building decks or external structures. From my standpoint, his father was intelligent and successful.

An added plus for the kid was that, when time afforded, he was able to work next to his dad and was learning the ins and outs of construction. He mentioned to me that he was able to build a deck on his own, and that adding on an extra room was no big deal.

This kid, though, has some pretty severe learning disabilities and was only able to read at a level much lower than his age would suggest. His math was also very substandard, but he excelled incredibly in art. Most of his peers were jealous of and intrigued by his ability to draw complex cartoon situations and caricatures. Clearly his example is of someone who has a lot of talents, but success in traditional schooling isn't one of them.

The discussion with his mother began along the lines of how to remedy his weaknesses. I mentioned that the reading and writing had to improve to be successful as an adult and that by allowing him to read whatever novels he chose would certainly help. I emphasized that it wasn't the content of the reading that mattered, but rather that he read anything at all. The vocabulary, I explained, and ability to spell accurately would surely follow.

Then, though, I directed the discussion towards his eventual adulthood, as this kid was in the ninth grade. We discussed his potential to excel in college, and what routes were open to him. I expressed the idea that anyone could excel in college, with enough effort, but that this particular kid had a huge opportunity to spend the next several years learning his father's trade, thus ensuring him an income as an adult. He showed an interest in construction, while showing a blatant disdain for traditional school. This, I went on, was a great option for this kid to be successful.

Surprisingly, though, I was met with anger. "Is my son not smart enough to go to college?" the mom blurted out. "Do you really want to limit him already?" she went on.

Genuinely surprised I tried to get to the bottom of her angst. I asked her if being a contractor was not successful. I asked her if I, with a college degree but earning on average less than successful contractors, was somehow better than contractors. After a few moments we found the common ground that we both wanted the boy to have a happy and successful life, but that we just weren't sure how to get there.

This example is a perfect one to show that parents have a predetermined notion of what success is. I am constantly tutoring kids in math and science who have parents that don't understand algebra but that have homes with pools, as they have found success through other means. Success, I would argue, is no longer as simple as going to college and living happily ever after. We as parents should be careful what we wish for and what we demand.

Included below is a rough list of some of the trades offered through these types of schools, take from the website (<u>http://www.</u>

rwm.org/rwm/tf cal.html ,) on 6/18/09. It is important to note that the entrance requirements into each trade varies, ranging from a B.A. in college to a high school diploma. What varies as well, obviously, is the length in time of the program and the cost. Some of these programs can be extremely expensive, as they lead to lucrative careers, while some are very affordable. Whatever the case, the list is formidable and is only a sample of all of the trades available. There are many more trades and trade schools available.

Aircraft: A&P Technician, Ground and Flight, Pilot
Arts & Design: Applied and Creative, Design, Media, Fashion
Automotive: Automotive Technician, Driver, Heavy Equipment Operator, Repair, Trucking
Bartending: Bartending Training
Business: Accounting, Administrative, General Office, Management, Marketing, Organizational Psychology, Secretarial
Computers & Information Technology: Computers & Information Technology: CAD, Installer, Multimedia, Programmer, Repairer, Web Designer
Construction: Estimator, Heavy Equipment Operator, Project Manager, Superintendent
Cosmetology, Barbering & Beauty: Esthetician, Cosmetologist, Hair Design, Facial, Make-Up, Manicuring, Nails, Salon Management
Criminal Justice: Corrections Officer, Security Guard
Culinary: Cooking, Baking and Pastry, Catering, Hotel and Restaurant Management, and more
Dental Assistant: Dental Assistant, Dental Administrator, Dental Receptionist
Digital Filmmaking and Multimedia: Digital Filmmaker, Video Editor, Sound Technician
Electronics & HVAC: Assembler, Electrical and Electronics Equipment Installer, Equipment Repairer, HVAC
Fashion Design: Apparel, Illustration, Merchandising
Gaming: Casino Dealer, Machine Repair, Table Games
Healthcare & Medical: Dental, Massage Therapy, Medical Assistant, Medical Office, Medical Records Technician, Nursing, Optician, Paramedic, Pharmacy Technician, X-Ray Technician

<u>Healthcare Office Management</u>: Office Management, Hospital Unit Coordinator

<u>Inspection & Environmental</u>: Hazardous Waste Technician, Home Inspection, Inspector, Quality Assurance

<u>Jewelry</u>: Bench, Designer, Identification, Diamond Setter

<u>Legal</u>: Court Reporter, Criminal Justice, Legal Office, Paralegal

<u>Machinist</u>: Machine Operator, CNC Machinist, CNC Operator

<u>Massage Therapy</u>: Massage Therapy Training, Massage Therapy and Health Educator Training

<u>Nursing</u>: Vocational Nursing, Registered Nursing, Nursing Assistant Training, Health and Rehabilitation Technician, Patient Care Assistant, and more

<u>Plumber</u>: Pipefitter

<u>Private Investigation</u>: Investigation, Security, Protection

<u>Rehabilitational Therapy</u>: Physical Therapist, Massage Therapist

<u>Secretarial</u>: Administrative Assistant, Computer Applications Specialist, Executive Assistant

<u>Telecommunications</u>: Assembler, Cable Installer, Fiber Optic Technician, Networking, Repairer, Systems Installer

<u>Television & Film</u>: Television Host, Producer, Anchorman, Anchorwoman

<u>Travel</u>: Flight Attendant, Hotel Management, Reservationist, Travel Agent

<u>Web Design & Web Management</u>: Web Designer, Web Developer, MCIWD

<u>Welding</u>: Pipe Welding, Welding Technology, Combination Welding

Whatever one's feelings about a four year education versus a more accelerated and directed learning experience, it is hard not to be excited by some of the above titles. For the less academic, flight attendant, private investigation, and gaming are just a few trades that are sure to raise an eyebrow, while the cranial types might be more interested in the aircraft field. The point is, trade schools deliver actual practical skills specific to certain careers rather than a more vague and all-encompassing education that some kids find deplorable.

So again, the case for trade schools is not made to devalue the larger university, as there is room for both to coexist. I personally feel as though my own time spent with the University of California, Santa Cruz was extremely valuable to me and it is something I would do again, if given the choice. What, however, I do regret is the time I spent unsuccessfully at CSU Chico, during which time the expenses were high and the rewards were low. My family, while loving and caring, was certainly guilty of giving advice congruent to the movement with the masses, shuffling me off to a college before I was ready. The two years immediately after high school might have been better spent, and at lower cost, in a tech school for immediate progress.

So, if a student is eager and ready for a large university, there are few things as wonderful. If not, however, one should cast aside their predetermined notions of what defines success, and allow for a more natural route to a productive life. It could very well be that a trade school is just that route.

CHAPTER 26: PARENT VERSUS TEACHER INFLUENCE

THE TYPE OF SCHOOL, HOWEVER, in no matter the form, is not the largest factor in determining the success of a child. At best, the high school or middle school setting can only be considered a secondary influence in the outcome of an individual.

What is either great news, or is a topic that would make a person nervous, is the magnitude of a parent's influence over their children. This influence that parents have over their children far outweighs that of any figure in the schools. This simple fact is responsible for why, on one hand, we have such amazing citizens in this country, yet is also the reason why some of the most dreadful people imaginable exist. Parental influence over a growing child has immeasurable power, but as with any source of power, it needs be treated with an equal amount of responsibility.

Historically, a selling point to a career in education has been the potential to affect lives and to essentially redirect those headed down the wrong path to a path of success. While other careers can offer greater monetary rewards, those with giving hearts were typically drawn to education for just this reason, the ability to help others. And while this potential influence on the lives of others is real, it has been overstated. Without question, it is parents that have a much larger influence on the character of kids than do teachers and school counselors.

Not only is the influence greater, it is greater by an apparently insurmountable amount. A source of frustration for teachers in every school district is the seeming inability to change kids for the positive because of some type of strife occurring at home. When the opposite is true, and a kid is supported at home and is in love with life, we, similarly, can accept very little of the credit for their success. The parents, in these cases, are the ones who set the stage for the success of the kid.

A famous rapper from the nineteen eighties had a controversial song which stated that if we wanted to end racism, we had to kill our parents. While obviously this is a vulgar and distasteful way to make a point, he hit the nail directly on the head. Most of our behaviors, good or bad, stem from our upbringing. Surely if someone's parents spoke of the evils of judging a person by race, the kid would grow up believing that racism is terrible, but if the parents promoted racially based hatred, the kid would grow up to be racist. This was the rapper's point.

Think of your values, from how you feel about animals or being outside to how you define happiness, and ask yourself if these themes may have come from your childhood and the values of your own family. Then ask if you are in the midst of creating those same values in your children. Well, while these are pleasant thoughts and actions, less than desirable traits and behaviors are passed along in much the same way.

I have had several students from the different schools that I have taught at that have referred to a relative in jail, with a less than ashamed tone. If kids are in the presence of violence and drug abuse for years on end, a ten minute lecture from a teacher about the ills of violence and drug abuse, no matter how clear, simply will have no effect. This is the frustration inherent in teaching and is the source of most of our problems as a society. For this reason, high performing schools versus poor performing schools are always a product of, not the ability of the staff and school, but the community itself.

And as to how the topic is relevant to our secondary schools and the plight of our teen-agers, policies in schools are inappropriately being designed at remedying this social dilemma. These kids are often being misdiagnosed as having performed poorly for some intellectual issue, when the problem is clearly social and or socioeconomic. If we can clearly identify that the direct factor in the failure of these kids is not the lack of creativity in curriculum, but due to the struggles they have at home, we can more accurately direct resources and influence.

Because low achievement is so much more prevalent in low income neighborhoods, despite the fact that there is no less ability intellectually, one has to wonder why. That is, what has come first, the irresponsible behavior or the poverty, because irresponsible behavior can certainly lead to poverty and the reverse is true as well. That is, if a person acts irresponsibly and has difficulties with the law, they often face the financial burden associated with court dates and fines. Also, they may lose jobs more readily, due to irresponsible actions, and will in the end be less productive financially.

As a specific example, a penalty for driving under the influence of alcohol, an irresponsible act, carries a hefty fine of thousands of dollars, which could put an individual behind financially for a few years. This type of repeated, irresponsible behavior would certainly lead to financial ruin.

Then, on the other hand, financial stress might, it could be argued, lead to irresponsible behavior. While this is not a new theme, and people have often expressed the need to commit crimes like theft and violence to merely survive in their neighborhood, I would argue that this is a perceived necessity rather than an actual one. I say this because, again, these behaviors seldom get a person ahead in terms of creating wealth, but push them further behind. Regardless, these actions may be a result of poverty and the stresses that come along with this lack of security. Whatever the case, this cycle is very sad.

It seems as though this cycle of coming from certain family circumstances or poverty and growing up to live in similar circumstances as an adult would be clear to the very kids involved in it and that they would put effort into ending it, but time and time again they do not. I have even quizzed troubled kids as to why they make the bad decisions they make, telling them that they are certainly limiting their futures with these actions, and their answers made it clear that they didn't understand that they were under the grips of a cycle. They simply understand a "norm" for their neighborhood and or family and continue in much the same way their parents may have acted in their childhood. It is nothing short of tragic.

These thoughts and discussions, though, have prompted me to try to find a solution to the statistical truth that people from bad situations overwhelmingly go on exist in bad situations as adults. In other words, I wonder if there is a way to break the cycle. Yet, it is this very cycle that offers the grand diversity in the world today. It is this cycle that produces fisherman, musicians, athletes, and business people. As long as we do as our parents do, we are assured as a society that we will fill every niche. And for families with the right priorities and the proper amount of care, this concept is beautiful. In the cases of the other kind, however, the reality is very sad.

If there were a way to start fresh, and assure that all kids were raised with love, care, and in a responsible fashion, we may be able to make a difference in the disparity between the rich and poor, and might make a dent in the crime in some of our rowdier neighborhoods. The answer to our societal woes are not through education and law enforcement, as they have had little effect, but through this simple idea of raising kids to see life as beautiful. There seems to be only one way to ensure that every kid is given a fair chance at a wonderful life, although slightly ludicrous and nearly impossible to implement.

We don't trust our citizens to drive without a license. Someone realized that it is simply too dangerous of an activity not to regulate. You also need a license to practice medicine, law, or to sell real estate. You need a license to fish; you need a license to be a chiropractor, to sell alcohol, and to collect salamanders from a local river. Some things are too consequential not to regulate.

Things that are not as inherently dangerous, however, don't require licensing, like flying a kite or riding a bike. So, at a certain point in the evolution of an activity, we as a people make a judgment as to what is potentially serious enough to necessitate licensing. When we as a society reviewed childbirth, then, we must have come to the slightly irrational decision that bringing another human being into our world fell into the latter category.

Is giving birth to and raising a human being such a light task that we should leave that simple endeavor up to the public at large, regardless of their situation, behavior, or ability to care for another? Apparently a real estate salesman without a license could do our society more harm than a homeless person having a baby. A fisherman without a license could do more to hurt us as a society than a violent father raising a child with his fists. Collecting salamanders irresponsibly would certainly hurt the United States of America more than a woman with a history of drug abuse and mental instability raising a few kids on her own.

Do you see the logic?

What if one had to apply for a license to become a parent and that the qualifications that we deem as important to being a good parent would have to be met before a license was granted? What if the potential parent had to demonstrate the ability to care for the child? What if the parent had to show that they would have a home for the child and that they didn't have a history of violence or substance abuse? The parent would have to do a little homework, much like we do before taking the written driver's test, before applying for the right to be a parent. If a person wasn't in the position to be a parent, what if they had to re-apply when they were in such a position?

This is obviously idealistic, but shouldn't some crimes automatically make an application void, like child molestation or child abuse. The local animal shelter put me through a grueling process to bring my Chihuahua home, including a letter from my landlord and pictures of my residence, while our first child was conceived without notice. The animal shelter made me swear that I would let my Chihuahua sleep inside, stating that little dogs don't like doghouses, while no one gave a single word to the creation of the most important thing in our lives.

And, with the adoption of my dog, a certain amount of reading and education was mandatory. Childbirth should be the same. Just as we have to cram to pass the driving test or adopt a Chihuahua, we should have to cram on information about raising a child before we are granted the license to have a baby. The test would include information like how to address diaper rash and how high of a temperature would necessitate the use of Tylenol. The test might also include some practical theories on how to deal with defiant behavior, as the child enters the toddler years. We as a society could determine what simple truths about parenthood should be universally known and put them on the required reading list. We do this for people to become realtors and bus drivers, and we should do it for people interested in becoming parents.

Maybe all applications wouldn't be cleared the first time, but the process would not be a one time thing. For instance, if a person did not have the proper circumstances to be able to provide for a baby, they would have to re-apply when they got their things in order. This again is similar to how most licensing agencies work today. Extreme poverty wouldn't be the limiting factor for someone interested in being a parent, but homelessness might be. The person would obviously have to tackle this issue of not having a roof over their head, before considering becoming a parent.

The irony is that this type of certification already happens with regards to becoming a parent, but only with adoption. Obviously the administrators of adoption organizations would never concede to simply having people drop by and pick up an infant without a proper investigation of the potential of the parents to care for another. They obviously have due diligence, both legally and morally, and look into the lives of the potential parents. There are certainly disqualifiers in this case, so I often wonder why the same process doesn't happen for biological parents. Once one thinks about the issue, it almost seems absurd that we don't already regulate who becomes a parent, just as is happening with adoption.

Imagine if we ran adoption centers in the same way that we do biological births. If this were the case, the doors would be wide open and anyone could swing by and grab a baby at random. Would you concede to having a woman with a terrible drug addiction and in a situation of extreme poverty just walk in and leave with an infant? Would you allow a drug dealer with several incidents of violence and gang relations waltz in and leave with a baby? How about a fourteen year old girl that is still in high school and isn't sure of who the father is, let alone who she is to become… would you let her come by and pick up a baby?

When the issue is put in reverse, in this way, the point becomes even more poignant. A person who ran an adoption center in this manner would likely be jailed for life, so one has to question why we treat children to be adopted with a higher amount of care than we do those that are conceived by biological parents.

I guess the question is really whether parenthood should be considered a privilege or a right. As is stated in the constitution of our great nation, your rights end where the rights of others begins. It only seems obvious that the right of a child to be raised in a situation that can allow for their healthy growth and eventual success would be a right that would supersede one's right to have that baby. How unlucky it would be to be born into a terrible situation, and how irresponsible of our society to allow such situations to unfold.

Obviously such a radical policy as licensing birth is laced with holes and would not be something we as a nation would swallow nor attempt to enforce, but the issue is thought provoking nonetheless. The majority of these ponderings have come from an experience that I had a few years ago, while my wife and I were doing everything in our power to make sure that every day for our two year old was a bright one.

I can remember working fourteen hour days and living frugally so that we would be able to afford a safe neighborhood for our little family as well as only greeting our little girl with kisses and smiles. In contrast, however, I would bike to work along the river and would occasionally pass a homeless woman on the levy with a baby.

Depending on the day, the baby would typically be laid out on a blanket, either naked or just in a diaper. Sometimes the baby would clearly have dirty diapers, and the baby would almost always be in a hysterical fit, showing extreme discomfort. One could plainly see rashes on the insides of the baby's legs and rear, and the general look of the baby was of poor health.

What was a constant, though, was what the mom was doing. When I would see her, she would always be in a circle with friends, all of whom were passing a pipe around the circle smoking pot. Obviously it isn't the fact that she was smoking pot that bothered me, but it was the fact that she would often have her back to the infant while she would get stoned with several other homeless people. The whole group was obviously transient and this baby was being raised amongst them, in the most terrible of situations.

Again, in contrast to what our little girl was receiving from us, how could one not be upset by what was being done to this little baby? And a good question would be why our baby deserved more than this one. Does this baby, being raised so poorly, deserve this? Was the baby to blame for anything? Simply because this child was born to the wrong person, they will go on to live a terribly difficult life, full of rough days and dark experiences. I can't fathom what nights are like for this baby, if the days are that bad. Can we as a society really stand for this type of injustice? Is the woman raising the baby the one who needs her rights protected, or is it those of the baby? I for one find this imbalance to be morally nauseating.

And looking at the larger picture, the issues that come up from being raised in a god awful situation are deep and many. Most violent criminals were raised in a violent home. Most child molesters report having been molested as a youth themselves. Most people that engage in gang activity have some influence from family members along those lines. It is certainly our parents who are to blame for many of the ills of the world.

From the point of view of a teacher, I can consistently anticipate what parents of students are going to be like by the behavior of their child. Teacher parent meetings are never a surprise to me, and I am always depressed to see that the bright and kind kids have bright and kind parents, while the angry and disinterested kids have angry and disinterested parents. The cycle is very real and, unfortunately, is too powerful for even the most compelling of teachers to break. Our influence as counselors and teachers can't hold a candle to the impact made in the home.

So, without question, we can assume that the cycle of violent people raising kids to become violent people will continue indefinitely. Former ideas, like extra education or extra law enforcement, have obviously not been proven successful. We still have a relatively large divide between the rich and the poor, and between safe and beautiful neighborhoods and poor and dangerous ones. Having taught in some pretty rough neighborhoods, I can attest to the fact that the cycle will not end with our current efforts.

As well, people being raised in such a manner constitute a huge economic drain on the nation with regards to social programs to support their activities. If one were to tally the extra funds needed to treat miscreant kids in schools, drug addicts in the clinics, foster programs for kids without supportive parents, prisons to house criminals, police to fight prevalent crime, welfare programs to feed low income families, and free healthcare programs, the bill would come to an astonishing amount. In the midst of the tax debate as President Barack Obama took office, a startling statistic mentioned was that the highest fifty percent of income earners in California pay ninety percent of the taxes. What the statistic didn't include is that the bottom fifty percent likely consumes the majority of that tax money through the aforementioned programs. How can this be sustainable?

So while I recognize the absurdity in trying to regulate child birth, the discussion is most valuable in that it pinpoints the problem. It appears as though the large gap between the rich and the poor will not disappear so far as people are able to bring children into this world regardless of their situation and so far as they are able to raise them with reckless abandon. We as teachers can only act as speed bumps to the process, in these cases, and if we can stop the cycle with even just a few kids, that is something to hang one's hat on.

Whatever becomes of our society along these lines, it is time we are candid about the source of struggle for these kids and that we stop proposing to fix the problem with mandatory office hours for teachers. No small change in curriculum or extra five minutes of support by a teacher will stand a chance to correct these deep rooted wrongs. More attention needs to be paid toward how we qualify "parents" in our society, and as long as adults can raise children with anger, abuse, and irresponsibility, the socioeconomic gap is here to stay.

CHAPTER 27: "PARENTS JUST DON'T UNDERSTAND"

To quote the very funny Will Smith song from the late eighties, "parents just don't understand." Even with the most caring parents in the world, with the best intentions, the stress that school brings to the dinner table today has provided a new source of friction for parents and kids. As a tutor, I have seen cases where, without the "on the ground" understanding of the situation, parents have quickly and unfairly measured their kids' performance. Specifically, without seeing the struggles and intense effort put into preparing for a test, the parent will see a low grade and immediately jump to the conclusion that the kids were either lazy or that they didn't try hard enough.

If parents analyze what they expect from their kid and ask how much of that expectation is within the control of their child, they would likely become more flexible on the subject. That is, should a person get an A, or should they study every night and try their best. The two can come hand in hand, but don't always. I have studied with countless kids for math tests and can testify that they might conceptually know ninety percent of the material, but then, because of some careless arithmetic, they might get a D on the test.

My response in this case is always to tell them to keep their head up and to start studying for the next one. I go on to yell at them to pay closer attention, with a smile, but don't see any productive outcome in showing sincere disappointment. After all, the student did study hard and knew much of the content, but they simply made mistakes. Grounding this kid or yelling at them can do nothing but harm and will likely lower their likelihood of performing better on the next test.

The intent from the parents in this case is completely kind in nature, as they only want their child to be successful and happy, but their efforts are a little misdirected. Either way, what I don't think should happen is that the stresses of the very heavy workload in our secondary schools be transferred into our relationship with our kids. There is nothing more important to us than our children, so it is sad that the ridiculous circumstances in our secondary schools could create strife between us and those very children.

Chapter 28: Homework Time

PROBABLY THE LARGEST CULPRIT FOR creating fights between parents and kids is homework. And while much of the blame sits squarely on the shoulders of schools and teachers that assign homework irresponsibly, there are some things that parents can do to make sure the process goes more smoothly.

The following are some directions for getting homework done on time and getting it done well. While homework might never be celebrated by your child, there are ways to make it less painful for them. The first step is to abandon whatever you have been doing up to this point, if getting homework done is like pulling teeth with your kid.

If you want to see how to do homework, look at the kids who do it without being told; college kids. First off, most college kids realize that, after a couple of bad grades, they can't do homework or any serious studying in their bedroom. The same goes for high school kids. I don't recommend that kids do their work in their room.

The number one reason that kids despise homework is not that it is hard, but that it is completely boring. It is torture for them to sit in a quiet kitchen, with the clock ticking, with the goal of tending to dry work from thick textbooks. If a parent is serious about having their kid be studious, homework has to be much more appealing than this. The first step in getting your kid to do homework is by making the whole experience attractive.

My tutoring center, in Santa Cruz, California, is a place that was designed specifically to ward off boredom. Many kids have mentioned, upon walking in, that "man, I didn't picture a tutoring center like this." I won't tutor a kid without music in the background, and the music isn't classical. We listen to everything from Jack Johnson and Damien Marley, to Bret Denin and The Shins. If you haven't heard of any of those bands, don't pick the music for your kids during study time.

I have reptiles all over the place and an electric guitar against one wall. I have funny books in a stack and will often take a break to show the kid a funny youtube video that another kid had shown to me. Is this a waste of valuable learning time? The answer is, not at all. By taking a little break to laugh or goof off, we get a much larger net amount of productive time studying than if we were to trudge along, eyes dry and backs sore.

Who can learn if they'd rather jump off of a cliff than do the assigned work? Let your kid listen to their headphones. Let them study at the beach or by the river. Let them study at a coffee shop; anything to keep the process fresh and fun. The kitchen table just isn't that fresh and fun.

Then, obviously only allow these freedoms on the condition of progress. I certainly am not condoning sitting by the river to sleep, but rather that it might elicit some creativity and work. And, because it is impossible for me to forecast what every kid in America prefers, with regards to a learning environment, allow your child to be a part of the selection process. Let them pick a spot. And just as I had to narrow down, in college, where I was and wasn't productive with my work, so will they. If they are wrong on their first guess, don't discard the notion that they should be able to pick their environment. Keep changing and trying new things until your kid has found a process and pattern that they do best in.

As a poignant example, writing a book requires a certain amount of both energy and fresh creativity. Without questioning the reason behind why the following fact was true, I found that I simply wrote more and was more creative in coffee shops than I would be at home. Fortunately, because I am an adult I can make the decision to go with what appears to work, I don't even sit down to write until I am in one of my favorite shops. If I had a tyrannical parent that said "too bad, work at the kitchen table," this book, for better or worse, would likely never have been written. And again, as stated above, I tried several places in which to sit down and write before I found the most productive situation. Allow these same freedoms to your kids if you truly are interested in having them find success.

So, again, while it is unlikely that ten college students have the same technique and the same location for studying, what they have in common is that it was their choice. And not only did they have the freedom to find an environment in which they worked best, it is unlikely that any of them got it right on the first try. Do not be afraid to give a little on the topic of the specific conditions under which homework is done, so long as the work does indeed get done. And in the end, if the kid is inspired, the quality of work will improve dramatically as well.

CHAPTER 29: ANY PASSION IS GOOD

WHAT IS INTERESTING WITH REGARDS to how parents and kids can fight is that the parents have nothing but love for the child, but that this reality is lost in translation. We only want success for our kids, but it may be that we are slightly narrow minded when it comes to the definition of success. I would argue that any success should be welcomed.

One kid that I tutor has been put in the classic category of a kid that is messing up in school. What is interesting about this kid, though, is that between the math problems we do together, this kid actually tutors me on engines and how they operate. I don't mean that he repeats something his dad has said in the garage but this kid is literally brilliant when it comes to engines and the accompanying parts. I call those particular parts "the accompanying parts," because I just have no idea of the names of the various wires, cords, and metal panels that inhabit the area under the hood. This kid does though.

In one of our first math sessions, he literally drew an engine and showed me the process of how a combustion engine takes the potential energy from gas and converts it into the mechanical energy that drives the car. If I had to label him as slow or accelerated; guess my choice? Not only does he know the names of parts, he can eloquently describe what role those parts have in the overall workings of a vehicle. Memorization is not impressive, but the total analysis of a machine and how it works is.

Never the less, he went on to school the next day to a series of disappointed gazes and brief but lame lectures from every teacher he faced. "If only he would put energy into his learning, he might get somewhere, etc." And this is the most dangerous thing about this whole school dilemma.

The kid is sharp enough to completely understand the workings of a motor. He is smart. But under the pressure of constant negative feedback, even the coolest of people begin to doubt themselves. I don't blame the teacher who fails to make a physicist out of every kid, but I blame the teacher who *tries* to make a physicist out of every kid.

We need to find these affinities, like the one described above, and push kids along in that direction. And if this doesn't happen in schools, parents, we need to correct that problem ourselves. If you are proud of your kid and know that he or she is passionate about life, downplay the grade updates and focus on what they are awesome at. If you know that your son or daughter is nuts about something cool, talk more about that than their math grade.

I remember another kid who was the captain of his ROTC crew, the best wrestler on his team and maybe in the city, was funny and great, but was getting a bad math grade. Of all the things listed, guess which topic was set in front of him at every moment from the drive to school to the discussion at the dinner table. You guessed it, the math grade. Could more time have been spent on giving this kid a pat on the back for the nineteen categories in which he was way above average? I told his dad that he should thank the lucky starts that this kid turned out so great, but he could only respond saying that a C- was hardly great.

Such a flagrant lack of listing priorities in their proper order is only a detriment to the kid involved and absolutely serves no positive end. All I could do when I saw that kid was to tell him how amazing his feats were. Of course we should bring the grade up, but we shouldn't bring the image he sees of himself down along the way. The discussions about what the kid does well should outweigh the bad by tenfold.

But these examples frame perfectly a different example of a kid who actually does need change. A kid that I worried about when I was tutoring him, was the one who was getting bad grades and appeared to have nothing to be excited about in any other facet of life, either. From computers and instruments to cars or sports, every kid needs something. This kid didn't have anything, and more alarming, didn't seem to be searching. After a few discussions with his parents, we began forcing the issue. If the kid doesn't search out passions for themselves, it is the responsibility of the parent to offer some ideas.

Having your cervix dilate to ten times its normal size, and or staying up at three in the morning to change the little shrimps diaper is not enough. We have to make sure that our kids find a love for life and a passion.

My kind mother had this in mind when she forced me to try out for the water polo team, and trust me when I say that she wasn't thanked for her efforts. The coach, who should be in prison for cruel acts to children, wanted me to carry a tire across the entire pool, using only my legs as the driving force. By the way, when a little water gets in a tire, do you understand how heavy those things are? Do you know how heavy those things are anyways? Oh yeah, and another cute little rule for water polo practice is that you can't hold onto the side of the pool until practice is over.

So that was a bad idea on my mom's end, as were many of her ideas, but if one of your ideas of twenty is good, you have just given your child a passion to hang onto for life. The story ends happily, as I owe my love for animals, my love of music, and my love for surfing to my dear and beautiful mother. See, you could read those words from your own child someday if you just keep trying.

The tale was dramatic, but the point is real. You are obviously not going to win with every idea you give your kid, but unless they find something on their own, you have the duty to keep trying. P.S. Knitting is making a comeback if you are looking for a starting point.

And for an explanation of why one would place such a high value on a passion or hobby, especially in the case that the passion wouldn't lead to an eventual career or source of income, it is the concept of success and self image. The positive feelings associated with success, no matter in what arena, is addicting and often spreads into other areas. We need something to hang our hat on, and if a kid can say that they are excellent at the saxophone, at chess, or in football, it gives them an anchor. Then, with such a positive self image, it is easy to begin to reach out and stand at the door of new challenges with a positive attitude.

For many kids, a great grade point average is just the success that I am describing and is awesome, but this should by no means the only thing that our kids can find to be proud of. With your guidance, your kid will find what they are great at, and no matter how mundane, absolutely encourage that endeavor.

CHAPTER 30: LET THEM FALL

WHO IS A BETTER KID, one that is accepted to medical school or one that flunked biology as a freshman in college? As the answer is obvious, the question seems a waste of time, but actually is being brought up to make a clear point. The two kids mentioned above are one in the same. I flunked biology my freshman year in college only to go on to get accepted to John A. Burns School of Medicine in Hawaii. I obviously didn't flunk because it was hard, but because I was the classic example of a disinterested kid. Having now worn both labels, that of the failure in school, and that of the success in school, I have a pretty interesting insight into what success is and what it requires.

When I began school as a freshman in college I did terribly. I was clearly the kid who would be frowned upon by neighbors as my family reluctantly told of my mishaps, and was probably written off by more people than I would like to imagine. Only later, when I found direction did I start to ace classes and go on to be accepted to medical school.

If you have a son or daughter in the predicament I described above, who appears to not be on track, I have some insight that might help. I don't blame the younger me for failing classes and "wandering." You couldn't have made me do well in school if you beat me with a stick (my mom tried that by the way.) If you are trying to lecture your kid into doing what is right, it will never in a million years work. As a parent you have to explain not to burp at the dinner table and to always use conditioner after shampoo, but when it comes to major life pursuits and direction, the motivation has to come from within.

Show your kid new things. Introduce them to new people. The famous line "the definition of insanity is doing the same thing and expecting different results" hits the nail on the head. Lecture after lecture will do nothing. A trip to Alaska, a cup of coffee with an old war veteran, or success in a new hobby or sport would make a change. These things actually have a shot at creating some change.

Kids need to see the world. Don't you love those movies where the little bear cub goes out and gets sprayed in the face by a skunk, only to go on to get stung by bees in a pursuit of some freshly brewed honey? Let your kid get stung. Let him or her get sprayed in the face by a skunk; tomato juice will remove that in a few weeks or so. The kids that I tutor express a huge desire to go out and prove themselves. A lot of them don't consider an A on a pop quiz the proof they were looking for. Why do you think all teenage boys rent those ridiculous "fight 'em up" movies? They are searching for a dangerous situation to barely get out of.

The invention of "teepee-ing" houses was not only to mess up a friend's lawn, but to create a simulation of what it feels like to run for your life. Which by the way, if you are reading this Mr. Jack, I almost had a heart attack when you came running out of your house with the maglite. That was not cool, Mr. Jack, not cool. Mission accomplished, we were running for our lives.

Again, these examples are not a plea for letting your kids drop out of high school only to live a risky life of vandalizing homes and school property, but to give you some insight into what is going on in their creative little minds. Armed with this knowledge, maybe you will be able to direct them towards some worthy challenges that won't result in you speaking with the local authorities. I sincerely believe that if your kid is acting confused and making horrible decisions, they are probably just looking for a wild adventure or for some direction in life.

Believe it or not, but the kid in high school that gets drunk and runs from the police is seen as a local hero at school the next day. If you aren't the best in baseball or successful in the band, you have to prove you can turn heads in some way. Some do it with hair color and some with daredevil events. Help your kid to find a way to turn heads in a healthy manner so that they won't feel compelled to do it in a destructive way. Piano lessons probably won't help, but giving them punk rock guitar lessons might. If you don't feel qualified to determine what will be cool to them, just ask another teen.

Run your idea by a neighbor kid, because if teenagers are nothing else, they are candid. Something I hear a lot from my tutoring kids is "that is soooooo stupid." If you get that response, you should try to get your money back for the accordion.

CHAPTER 31: NAGGING

OW MOMS, I CAN FEEL your shoulders tensing up and can see you putting on your defensive "look," but don't worry, this is not a personal attack. You know, that may be the best part of giving information through a book, in that no one feels as though they are being personally targeted, as it is impossible for me to know who will be reading this. You are off the hook. That is, unless you gave birth to me, in which case you are my mom and you should feel free to take this as a direct attack. And actually, the content for this chapter wasn't created as much as a response to my own childhood but in response to the speeches I have watched my students endure over the years from their parents.

Why don't banks nag? That is, when you overdraw, do you get a call from a woman in her late thirties or early forties crying out "you know, you can't keep doing this. I told you soooo many times that overdrawing is irresponsible and is such a hassle for us here at the bank. Do you care about us? You seem so selfish when you do that. We work hard to send you checks when you run out, we offer you coffee when you come in and how do you thank us? By overdrawing? When are you going to grow up?" Do you see where I am going with this?

No, the bank simply stings you with a certain fee and they leave it up to you to decide if the penalty is worth overdrawing periodically. There is no emotion. If you don't mind paying the $50 penalty fee, then continue overdrawing at your leisure. If the penalty is too great, you had better stop overdrawing. Banks don't nag and they get great results. Of course, there should be a little more warmth in the home than in a bank and the definition of a mother is someone who is forgiving, but if you aren't getting the results you had hoped for, just look to your local bank for parenting advice. They seem to be pretty good at it.

It might also be smart to identify what will and won't work based on what requires nagging in the first place. In other words, the necessity to nag can be a measure for whether or not an activity is going to stay around. For instance, if you have to nag your child to practice the piano; the chances are, sorry to say, that they will not go on to play for the rest of their lives. When you hear of children that go on to be musicians, it is almost always the case that, along the way, it was actually hard to keep them away from the instrument.

One of my kids plays drums, and the parents had never told him to practice. According to them, once he sat down for the first time, his interest in the instrument took off like wildfire. Four hundred hours later, which seemed like no time at all to both the kid and his parents, he is playing like an expert. If you ask him how much he practices, he responds with a confused look. According to him, he doesn't practice, but simply plays for a couple of hours a day, or whenever he gets the chance to.

Another kid we know, was given drums for Christmas, played them for a few months, and moved on. The point is that in the second case, nagging or no, the child was not going to embrace the drums. So, rather than try to make happen what will certainly not, it is good to measure the "fit" of an idea by how much nagging is required to keep it afloat. Once the nagging starts, the battle has pretty much been lost.

If your family determines that something is worth fighting for, don't consider nagging an option. To create real results you'll need to develop incentives and, unfortunately, your own version of "late fees." I tried pleading with my two year old and even gave lengthy explanations as to why calling her older sister "bad dirl," (she can't pronounce her G's yet,) wasn't nice, but got no results. Only after the sentence of a two minute "time out" did she begin to contemplate whether or not it was worth it to keep saying that little phrase. I got the idea from my local bank.

CHAPTER 32: VIDEOGAMES

I DON'T KNOW THE FOLLOWING FROM personal experience, but I think it is safe to say that avoiding crack to begin with is easier than quitting crack after the habit has begun. Is this analogy too extreme to use for video games? I think not. The only way to completely avoid the inevitable waste of a huge portion of one's life to video games is to never begin them in the first place.

If you don't understand why kids play video games for so many hours on end, just try a game yourself. Those games are unbelievably fun. I remember mocking one of my students, only to go on to try the game they were praising. Thirty five minutes later my grin was half the size of my face and I had to hit "exit" only to go on to eat a meal. I honestly thought about skipping the meal, to just make that little bit of progress needed to get to the next level of the game, but fearing that I'd be labeled the class one hypocrite, I left the device behind. After a case of the shakes and some sweating, I think I've gotten over the experience.

So I may have exaggerated a little, but the fact is that those games are amazingly addicting. If you don't want your child to sit in a poorly lit room and stare at a screen for hours on end, say "no" when they ask for a video game machine for Christmas. You might not win a subsequent popularity contest, but in the end you'll be helping the little guy or girl. I've heard the quote "it is so realistic," countless times and always wonder why, if the aim is to reach a level of realism don't the kids just go out and play the "real" game. "The Wii tennis game is so close to the real thing," they say, so I can't comprehend why they wouldn't just go out and play tennis.

If you have let things go, though, and you have an addict on your hands, there is little that can be done. Once a kid has had the taste, it is hard to reverse the process. I bet after an exciting trip to wilderness camp, though, they might not go as crazy when you put

196 | *Ryan Teves*

the machine in the trash. I could be wrong and I will deny that it was my idea if things go bad.

The scary thing is that the kids who were the original population to become addicted to video games are no longer kids. I know people that are now thirty two years old that wait in line at four in the morning for a video game machine. Knowing this might be a real possibility with your kids, I'd rather handle a battle with a thirteen year old than a thirty year old. Even though the fight won't be pretty, I would argue that it is a fight worth having.

The good news, though, is that it just isn't true that these games can somehow brainwash our kids into becoming violent or weird. It would make sense that they might, but I watched cute little kids navigate a series of rooms in a video game machine gunning hundreds of "bad guys," only to stop and go on to tell me how they think butterflies are pretty. I don't think the games are as much about killing things as they are about doing whatever task is required in the nanosecond that you have to do it. This might explain why games like super Mario brothers, basically peaceful, are as successful as fight games.

So while your kids won't be brainwashed into going on rampages, they will lose a shocking number of hours of their time here on earth to a literally fruitless endeavor. I always ask my tutoring kids if they play an hour of video games per day, and most will say that an hour is a low estimate. I then go on to tell them that I guarantee that if they spent an hour a day on guitar they could be as good as the punk bands they listen to by the time they graduate from high school. While this is absolutely true and should be a life-changing piece of information, I usually only get a single raised eyebrow if I've delivered the speech exceptionally well that day, and then the kids go on to play the same video games that night.

I remember a few years ago, my cute little cousin at the time asked for a few quarters to play a game before the movie we had just paid for was to begin. Most of these games have a little pregame video rolling, to hook the kid with the most quarters and to give a taste as to what the game might be like. The game we planted in front of for the little sales pitch video seemed normal enough at first, but what the three of us then witnessed was appalling.

The game had a man in his thirties talking to us, delivering some important and top secret details about a mission, while from about ten feet behind the man a bad guy was slowly creeping up. Despite our cries of warning, the bad guy approached without being detected. Then, as the villain got right up behind the man, he raised a hatchet, and chopped the guy in the back of the head. The man talking to us looked shocked, in some pretty intense discomfort, and then fell to the ground.

I'm not sure what the game was about or why the guy got chopped in the head, but my cousin was sold and shouted "this one!" Apparently the videogame makers had done their due diligence and pretty much "got" what kids like.

Did we give him the quarters? For the sake of suspense and in the nature of any good thriller, I'll have to not answer that question. But, my cousin is a sensitive and healthy young man to this day, which supports the idea that, while these games are sick and wrong, they do little actual damage to the person playing them.

Now, along the lines of how the nicotine patch is supposed to work, you might get away with weaning the alleged addict off of the games. There is obviously a huge discrepancy between games and how disgusting they are. As a service to the parent consulting with Santa about this year's potential Christmas gifts, I'll give you the limited understanding that I've picked up from kids around town.

One game, called "Grand Theft Auto" is basically a game in which you go around town murdering and plundering, except in a modern day setting. There is some sort of story line that you follow, but if you choose to stray from that, you can simply steal cars from innocent people, kill women and children, shoot at police, and pretty much do whatever weird and impulsive action you'd like. I guess the thrill is in being able to do what you obviously wouldn't be able to, or hopefully wouldn't want to do in real life. Either way, you might leave this one off of the list. As for a rating from the kids, they love it.

On the more decent end, though, there are games that basically reenact real historical events, and could arguably be called mildly educational. One of my kids just got a game that is about world war D and stages real battles with the actual names of the leaders, cities, and nations involved. Then, as a compromise and in an attempt to throw a bone to the kids, the game of course delivers the usual gratuitous blood and fire, sticking with the back alley agreement between kids and video game makers that took place some time in the past.

Then, approaching perfect, there are even better games that take thought and productive focus. There is one game in which you have to build a city, taking into consideration traffic concerns, police and fire support, and revenue creating facilities like sports stadiums, etc. The game then moves forward and there can be civil unrest due to poor infrastructure, or the occasional natural disaster to test your city planning. It actually sounds pretty cool. So, sticking with the analogy, this sounds like the proverbial nicotine patch we were looking for. This being said, though, I'd rather not have my kids try crack to begin with than to try to wean them off of it down the road. Say NO to video games.

Whatever one's approach to finding success for their child may be, understanding as much about their situation as possible is an important part in creating fair and intelligent policies. I have been fortunate, through my tutoring business, to have worked with sweet, caring, and brilliant parents that have had nothing in mind but giving their kids the head start they'll need to have a fulfilling and wonderful life. With this type of home-life, these kids are all but guaranteed happiness and success.

This being said, I still feel obligated to send out the warning signal that the stresses of our secondary schools are creating unnecessary fighting at home. Look, with an attention to detail, at the policies of the teachers and the school itself before assuming that the student is entirely to blame. It is true that kids are often times resistant to doing what it takes to get the perfect grades, but a little research into "why" might help. School has some serious problems, and until those are corrected, some empathy for what our kids are dealing with would certainly help at the home front.

Chapter 33: The solution: 2 pillars

ECAUSE WE HAVE BEEN DOING things the same way for such a long time, the woes of our secondary schools seem deep and unmovable, but the opposite is true. We have some of the brightest kids in the world, some of the brightest teachers, and plenty of resources in a country that enjoys the highest standard of living on the planet. In reality, the majority of the complaints of kids and parents would disappear with the addressing of the two major problems in school, and a fundamental shift in thinking about what education is. The solution to the struggle of our secondary schools to both educate and inspire our teenagers is based on two fundamental principles.

These two pillars moving forward, that should be prioritized above all else, would be those of individualization and relevancy. If we were to make policies with these in mind, all else would work itself out. These two basic ingredients have made junior colleges wildly successful, while their absence has crippled our middle and high schools.

To employ these concepts, the plan of action would be as follows. To allow for room for this individualization and to address relevancy, the first step would be to decrease the list of mandatory classes for graduation, but not the number of classes, total. That is, the same number of years and credits would be required to graduate, but there would be greater flexibility in how a student reaches that number.

First off, we would only make classes mandatory if they are deemed to be essential to adult life in America. Every kid would have to be able to read and write, as well as be able to perform math associated with survival in our society. No math above and beyond that of the daily interactions of the business world would be required for graduation. As well, a certain amount of history, and other courses would be mandatory, again, aimed at creating a bright and involved citizen.

Then, because these standards will have been met in the first or second year of high school, branching out into specialties can begin to happen, thereafter. While the route of continuing with higher learning would absolutely still be offered to those interested in college, as is seen today, other routes would also be offered from this early point on. Just as is seen in community colleges, kids would be able to pursue a skill or trade that would lead to a paying job upon graduation, if they desired.

Calculus and AP Chemistry would remain on the course list, but in addition one would see medical assistant, beautician, electrician, and dental hygienist. The list would offer room for individualization, would be relevant, and would, importantly, excite the kids. Rather than worrying about whether or not we are offering "intellectual" jobs or "remedial" jobs, there would certainly be a range. Rather than judge or place these niches on a ladder of worthiness, we should offer them all and let the kids follow the path of their interest.

It seems that only in the most dire of situations are we allowed to be creative. Currently there is a program called "the job core" in which they offer classes just like the above to high school dropouts. The kids take "programs" in the morning, consisting of classes like "framing houses," "cement," and "solar panel installation." They then go on to take academic classes in the afternoon, including math and English. If a kid fails, only then are educators given the room to be more flexible with curriculum. Do we have to wait until a student drops out of high school to be able to offer them the option to follow automotive technology or house framing?

So if we focus on the two priorities of relevancy and individualization, creating secondary schools that are embraced by our kids will be easy. As community colleges are not criticized for creating socioeconomic gaps, but rather are celebrated for offering practical skills, so will secondary schools be. Setting up a sink or swim situation, as exists today in schools, is more culpable for creating stratification in our society than the offering of multiple routes for success.

NOT EVERY KID WANTS TO GO TO COLLEGE. As long as we deny this simple fact, and make policies along those lines, we will never begin to serve this huge percentage of our population. And for those that do desire to move onto college, their learning up until now has been negatively impacted by the large group of discontented students, reluctantly sitting in desks around them. Forcing students in directions against their will is un-American and is a detriment to every kid in the system.

And as a part of the solution and of the execution of the solution, a focus on higher efficiency and the elimination of much of the red tape and bureaucracy would need to be a high priority. The solution, with its flexibility, would be expensive, so wise and well aimed spending would be important and the cumbersome hurdles associated with becoming a teacher would have to be diminished or removed. And while some of the largest areas of waste in schools were already discussed, there are countless other small pockets of waste that would have to be eliminated, while implementing the plan above.

And to address the real concerns as to our competitiveness around the world, a shift in thinking has to happen. In Barack Obama's state of the union address, on January 28, 2010, there was mention that we must improve our performance in math and science for our students to remain competitive around the world. Currently our scores are less than impressive. If President Obama, or any president for that matter, were serious about remaining competitive around the world in math and science, he would endorse the above proposed solution.

By not forcing students in a direction that they resist and resent, the students that are involved with the higher math and science classes would be enthusiastic, motivated, and would have a sense of accomplishment. The math classes would no longer be weighted down by disinterested students, but would be a collection of the most ambitious. This would only lead to much greater success among our students that are interested in math and science.

Think, again, of the approach of a professional football team. Never did they think that to create an elite team of finely tuned football players, it would be a good use of their resources to train every single person in America to run the fifty yard dash faster. They would never invest in having every single member of our nation on a weight lifting regimen, so that the average weight lifting capability would increase. This is obviously absurd.

Rather, professional football teams recruit. They find people that show both an ability and affinity for the sport, natural or learned, and invest tenfold in just those individuals. While many teams are famous for investing in athletic fields in the inner cities to promote the sport in general, the majority of their directed efforts are aimed at those who will most likely show positive results.

If we in America were serious about dominating in math and science, we would follow a similar plan. Having the entire average of the whole nation on math and science tests go up by two points does nothing for innovation or leadership in these areas. It is obviously the top five percent that will be making real change. Because of this simple fact, we as a nation should stop considering the "mean" test score on a standardized test to be such a critical piece of information. The average test score for all persons in our country absolutely has no value in assessing our place in the world.

So, because the proposed solution would address the majority of the concerns of all parties involved in the education process, it seems to make perfect sense. We would see greater participation amongst the underserved populations, those previously headed to universities will still do so, our high school graduates will either have an employable skill or the skills to move on to college, and our competitiveness around the world would be greatly increased. And because the premise for this whole book is that things are not working well as they stand now, some real change needs to happen sooner rather than later. This change can't be tiny and corrective in nature, but a major shift in thinking about what education is.

In a situation in which a large majority of kids are disappointed with our secondary schools, we can't think that the status quo is okay. Our kids are kind, bright, and creative, and deserve to be worked with instead of worked against. Let's adopt a model that works and discard the model that doesn't. With my own daughters, it is heart breaking to think that for those critical years of their development that they will have to put their individuality and passion aside, in order to follow some predetermined path of the masses.

No longer should we try to repress the energy and creative individuality seen in our teens, but rather, we should harness it. The desire of our kids to pursue deep and relevant learning about the world around them, as well as their desire to be unique individuals is not something we should frown upon, but something we should endorse. Let's be proud of the American teen.

Glod, Maria. "U.S. Teens Trail Peers Around World on Math-Science Test", Washington Post Staff Writer, Wednesday, December 5, 2007, Taken from the internet on 3/30/10, <http://www.washingtonpost.com/wpdyn/content/article/2007/12/04/AR2007120400730.html>

WebMD Medical Reference in collaboration with The Cleveland Clinic, Edited by Charlotte E. Graveson, MD., June 2004, Medicinenet.com Taken from the internet on 1/28/09 <http://www.medicinenet.com/script/main/art.asp?articlekey=41895>

StudentMarket.com, Inc., 8 Faneuil Hall Marketplace, 3rd Floor, Boston, MA 02109 Taken from internet on: 5/23/09 <http://www.studentmarket.com/aboutsat.html>

Rotherman, Andrew J. "Ensuring High Quality Education for Students with Special Needs," -*Testimony before the Senate Appropriations Subcommittee for the District of Colombia, April 16, 2002.* PPI Progressive Policy Institute, www.ppionline.org Taken from the internet on 4/15/2010, <http://www.ppionline.org/ppi_ci.cfm?knlgAreaID=110&subsecID=900030&contentID=250389>

"Per Student Cost Figures for The District of Columbia Public School System" by Mary Levy and, Washington Lawyers' Committee for Civil Rights & Urban Affairs, November 2007, Taken from the internet on 4/15/2010. <http://www.21csf.org/csf-home/DocUploads/DataShop/DS_86.pdf>

Witmer, Denise. "ADD and ADHD Statistics" -Your Guide to Parenting of Adolescents *CDC Report Looks at Attention-*

Deficit/Hyperactivity Disorder Taken from internet on 12/31/09. <http://parentingteens.about.com/cs/addadhd/a/add_stats.htm>

RWM Vocational Schools Database. Taken from the internet on 6/18/09. http://www.rwm.org/rwm/tf_cal.html

Brian Gill, policy analyst, Rand Corp.; and Steven Schlossman, head of History Department at Carnegie Melon University. "HISTORY OF HOMEWORK," the San Francisco Chronicle, Sunday, December 19, 1999. www.sfgate.com. Taken from the internet on 12/10/09, http://www.sfgate.com/cgi-bin/article.cgi?f=/e/a/1999/12/19/NEWS4357.dtl

"Homework?, Should We Lengthen The School Year?, Paths To Work: Vocational Education." Taken from the internet on 12/12/09. http://social.jrank.org/pages/992/Trends-in-Elementary-Secondary-Education